GREATNESS CODE

ALAN C. GUARINO

GREATNESS CODE

The Formula Behind Unstoppable Success

WILEY

Copyright © 2026 by John Wiley & Sons, Inc. All rights reserved, including rights for text and data mining and training of artificial intelligence technologies or similar technologies.

Published by John Wiley & Sons, Inc., Hoboken, New Jersey.
Published simultaneously in Canada.

No part of this publication may be reproduced, stored in a retrieval system, or transmitted in any form or by any means, electronic, mechanical, photocopying, recording, scanning, or otherwise, except as permitted under Section 107 or 108 of the 1976 United States Copyright Act, without either the prior written permission of the Publisher, or authorization through payment of the appropriate per-copy fee to the Copyright Clearance Center, Inc., 222 Rosewood Drive, Danvers, MA 01923, (978) 750-8400, fax (978) 750-4470, or on the web at www.copyright.com. Requests to the Publisher for permission should be addressed to the Permissions Department, John Wiley & Sons, Inc., 111 River Street, Hoboken, NJ 07030, (201) 748-6011, fax (201) 748-6008, or online at http://www.wiley.com/go/permission.

The manufacturer's authorized representative according to the EU General Product Safety Regulation is Wiley-VCH GmbH, Boschstr. 12, 69469 Weinheim, Germany, e-mail: Product_Safety@wiley.com.

Trademarks: Wiley and the Wiley logo are trademarks or registered trademarks of John Wiley & Sons, Inc. and/or its affiliates in the United States and other countries and may not be used without written permission. All other trademarks are the property of their respective owners. John Wiley & Sons, Inc. is not associated with any product or vendor mentioned in this book.

Limit of Liability/Disclaimer of Warranty: While the publisher and author have used their best efforts in preparing this book, they make no representations or warranties with respect to the accuracy or completeness of the contents of this book and specifically disclaim any implied warranties of merchantability or fitness for a particular purpose. Certain AI systems have been used in the creation of this work. No warranty may be created or extended by sales representatives or written sales materials. The advice and strategies contained herein may not be suitable for your situation. You should consult with a professional where appropriate. Further, readers should be aware that websites listed in this work may have changed or disappeared between when this work was written and when it is read. Neither the publisher nor authors shall be liable for any loss of profit or any other commercial damages, including but not limited to special, incidental, consequential, or other damages.

For general information on our other products and services or for technical support, please contact our Customer Care Department within the United States at (800) 762-2974, outside the United States at (317) 572-3993 or fax (317) 572-4002.

Wiley also publishes its books in a variety of electronic formats. Some content that appears in print may not be available in electronic formats. For more information about Wiley products, visit our web site at www.wiley.com.

Library of Congress Cataloging-in-Publication Data is Available:

ISBN: 9781394361595 (cloth)
ISBN: 9781394361601 (ePub)
ISBN: 9781394361618 (ePDF)

Cover Design: Jon Boylan
Cover Image: © Ekasan/stock.adobe.com
Author Photo: © Guido Venitucci

SKY10127793_100625

Dedication

Leadership is an AWESOME responsibility that, sadly, is often practiced poorly. I know because I have been in the leadership field since my days studying at the world's premier leadership school—the U.S. Military Academy at West Point—and then later as a practitioner in various businesses.

In my job, I too often hear from passionate, talented individuals working for people who suck the oxygen out of a room. These are people who fail to inspire or appreciate the awesome responsibility that comes with being a leader.

This book is dedicated to everyone who has worked in a tough environment for incapable leaders who derail talented careers. Fortunately, despite these poor leaders, many individuals persist and move forward. When the work environment becomes untenable, they pivot in new directions, and with courage, persistence, stamina, resilience, and passion, along with a strong social capital network—they prevail. These are individuals who achieve their Greatness Objectives.

This book is equally dedicated to the GREAT leaders who are authentic. Leaders who understand they have an *awesome* responsibility. Let's remember the people they lead are someone's mom, or son, or daughter, or dad, or neice, or nephew, or cousin - real people with feelings and goals. People who others depend upon. The happiness, broader mental health, and the livelihood of these employees are squarely in the leader's hands. Think about that for a minute. Wouldn't you agree that those are some of the most important components of the human condition? The impact of leadership is massive. Others' lives truly depend on it.

Contents

Acknowledgments — ix
Preface: A Note About Leadership — xi
About the Author — xvii
Introduction — xix

PART I Early Stage: Laying the Foundations — 1

Chapter 1   Early Challenges Will Build the Right Muscles — 3

Chapter 2   The 5 Qualities (5Qs) in the Face of Early Career Challenges — 37

Chapter 3   Establishing Social Capital Early — 45

Chapter 4   Early-Stage Exercise: Build Your Foundation and Launch Your Career — 59

PART II Mid-Career: Maximizing Momentum — 65

Chapter 5   Leveraging Social Capital for Advancement — 67

Chapter 6   Cultivate Lasting Grit — 81

Chapter 7   Mid-Career Exercise: Reassess, Stay the Course, or Realign Your Path — 91

PART III   Career Peak: Sustain Success and Leave a Legacy — 97

Chapter 8 Navigating Leadership with Grit and Social Capital — 99

Chapter 9 After the Summit: Building a Legacy through Social Capital — 113

Chapter 10 Sustaining Success through Continuous Growth and Adaptability — 121

Chapter 11 The Power of a Legacy Defined by Grit and Social Capital — 139

Chapter 12 The Balance of Grit and Well-Being — 151

Chapter 13 Peak-Career Exercise: Hone Your Final Approach and Envision Your Future — 159

PART IV   Post-Career: Coming Down the Mountain After the Peak — 165

Chapter 14 Deciding If, When, and How to Retire — 167

Chapter 15 Public Company Board Service: A Step-by-Step Guide — 179

Chapter 16 Engage with Private Equity and Venture Capital: A Post-Career Opportunity — 183

Postscript — 191
Epilogue The Brain's Evolution: From Striving to Thriving as You Come Down the Mountain — 197
Bibliography — 203
Index — 215

Acknowledgments

This book would not have happenned without all I have learned and been given from family, friends, clients and colleagues. To my friends you know who you are. *I thank you.* Perhaps you grew up with me in Danbury, Connecticut, or at West Point. Or you shared my life in Marlboro, New York; or New York City; or Fort Knox, Kentucky, or you are a client or colleague who became a friend.

To Kathy: We have been on life's journey for two-thirds of my life. I thank God for that. You wisely stop me whenever I head the wrong way—because you can see around corners. You have supported me in taking big risks. You built and sold a company with me. You helped me mold my career while striving and succeeding on a career journey of your own. Most importantly, you raised our children and are the nucleus of our family. Without you, nothing happens. YOU ARE MY *GREATNESS CODE.*

To My Children: You have given me a front-row seat to the challenges and opportunities Millennials face. Thank you for your guidance and wisdom. Boomers like me can easily misunderstand what the playing field looks like for your generation. You both AMAZE me with your work ethic and empathy for others. Thank you for standing on your own two feet.

To My Sisters: I read a magazine cover story that explored how your siblings make you who you are. I never doubted that my older sisters, Amy and Marie, made me who I am. They filled me with confidence and attention. They told me very clearly when I got a little full of myself. They showed me where the limits were. They were the first generation in our family to graduate from college, then on to master's degrees, and postgraduate work. They set the example for me. They are the best kind of winners—the ones who speak with their actions.

To My Parents: My mom showed me *the way* in her faith in God and Family, while my dad showed me how to work hard, *like it or not*. They were two of the most amazing people God ever created. They were the best role models—devoted, humble, smart, caring, and honest. They didn't have an easy road. I will never match their success.

ACG

Preface
A Note About Leadership

Before we can explore how individuals working within organizations pursue their personal *Greatness Objectives*, we must first acknowledge the critical role of organizational leadership. We explore the notion of a Greatness Objective in detail throughout this book. For now, I'll summarize it by noting that it is a success goal that an individual self-defines and strives for in work and in life. At any given time, people will have multiple Greatness Objectives they are striving for. To achieve their objectives, they need five key *qualities*: Stamina, Courage, Resilience, Passion, and Persistence, (SCRPP)—the 5Qs. They also need social capital, which is the golden circle of people who provide you leverage in various ways.

No matter how talented or driven a person may be, their ability to achieve greatness is significantly influenced by the culture, structure, and direction established by those at the top. Leadership sets the tone, defining not just what success looks like, but also how people are expected to show up, collaborate, and grow. Great leaders create the conditions for others to excel. They remove barriers, provide clarity, and build trust. Without strong, intentional leadership, even the most ambitious individual may find themselves operating in an environment that stifles rather than supports their potential. In contrast, when leadership is aligned with purpose and people-centric values, the organization becomes a fertile ground for personal and collective greatness.

I recently had a conversation with Jeff Sprecher that deeply resonated with me. Jeff is the Chairman and CEO of Intercontinental Exchange (ICE). ICE owns the New York Stock Exchange and other important financial companies. Jeff founded ICE and epitomizes the 5Q elements of the Greatness Code. Why do I say this? While launching the company, Jeff and his team solicited 106 potential institutional customers with no success. That's right; they were rejected 106 times and continued to push ahead. The 107th potential client they approached offered to get involved. That client was Goldman Sachs. I'd say that story exemplifies the 5Qs and how they can lead to greatness.

Jeff has articulated how the top leadership teams set up a company to empower employees and take on the awesome responsibility of leadership. He made his points with clarity and conviction. Jeff emphasized that the environment people work in is either an enabler or an obstacle to high performance. And that environment—its tone, its standards, and its sense of possibility—is shaped almost entirely by the culture instilled by the leadership team. He believes that leaders must be intentional in designing a culture that empowers people to take risks, grow, and thrive. Without that foundation, no amount of individual ambition will be enough. Leadership is the starting point for individual and organizational greatness.

Jeff says that he and his team achieve this through very deliberate actions. Each week his executive team meets for four hours. Their well-engineered approach encourages discord and open and honest communications among these key stakeholders. They are not required to stay in their lanes. They can address issues across all businesses and functions. They are open and authentic. At the end of the four-hour session, they either come to an agreement, or they table the matter until the following week. There are no "meetings after the meeting" or "meetings before the meeting" that would foster the dynamic of corporate politics. Instead, they work through the issues until they reach consensus. Then, they all get on board and support the decision. The leaders take this open and honest communication to their own units and replicate it several levels down into the organization. People feel they have a say. And people have information, so they understand why and how decisions are made.

During an interview, "Inside the ICE House" ICE's official podcast hosted by Josh King in May 2020 and marking ICE's 20th anniversary, Jeff and Josh King explored the company's transition from a nimble startup to a global marketplace powerhouse. During the interview, Jeff recounted how he and Chuck Vice, the ICE president at the time, worked to refine ICE's culture to ensure their employees had a great platform:

> "I will tell you that, for years, what Chuck and I have been working on is our culture, trying to figure out exactly what made us so successful and how do we enshrine that inside the company so that the company is bigger than any one individual including Chuck or [me]."

Leading requires honesty, vulnerability, and great communications skills. People are poorly led when leaders say one thing and do another. That creates a culture of mistrust. Great leadership fosters engaged employees who feel they have a chance to attain their personal Greatness Objectives while also delivering for their organization. That type of culture is key.

I want to share one more example. I have known Robin Vince for more than 15 years. We met during the 2008 financial crisis when he was a board member at a financial institution that needed to reorganize. I had the opportunity to help with that reorganization. Now, I have the opportunity to work closely with him in his role as Chairman and CEO at BNY.

Robin has made culture a centerpiece of his transformation strategy at BNY—and an important, bold move was making every eligible employee a shareholder. In December 2022, he launched the "BK Shares" program, granting 10 Restricted Stock Units (RSUs) to BNY employees. Robin described the move this way:

> "We all contribute to BNY's positive outcomes, and equity participation is an important way to feel connected to our growing value. . . . It's especially meaningful that, with this new program, many employees will become first-time participants in the very capital markets we help power."

In a later interview with *Time*, he reinforced the rationale behind this move: "So we made everybody a shareholder. So now, not only are employees theoretically excited about the journey, they're economically excited about the journey as well."

This wasn't just a gesture of goodwill—it reflected an intentional cultural realignment as well as a broader effort to create a sense of ownership at every level of the organization. Robin emphasizes that culture isn't a soft concept; it's a strategic lever.

The equity initiative is part of a larger philosophy rooted in authenticity, accountability, and communication. Robin has said:

> "Leadership depends on inspiring people at every level to help move an organization forward, creating a culture of transparency with consistent, actionable feedback, and empowering those around you to act as owners. Forming a network of doers across businesses, regions and functions is as much about commercial outcomes as it is cultural ambitions."

This mindset has enabled him to lead a company-wide shift away from siloed, legacy structures toward a unified, client-focused platforms model. This change in direction required clearly articulating a vision for the company and distilling the strategy into a simple format—pillars and principles. Three pillars that clearly outline BNY's strategy, and five principles that define how employees should show up each day. Employees now share a clearer sense of purpose and cohesion—understanding not only *what* BNY does but *why* it matters and *how* they each contribute to it.

Thus far, the cultural transformation has also produced tangible business results. Under his leadership, BNY's stock has climbed significantly, the company has delivered record earnings, and it continues to be recognized by *Fortune* as one of the world's most admired companies. But more importantly, the internal momentum has shifted. A focus on fostering a high-performing and human culture means employees are not just working for a new BNY—they're building it.

High performance doesn't happen without being front-footed. Robin has said,

> "Innovation is core to the DNA of BNY—companies do not last 240+ years without continuously re-inventing themselves. I see a certain freedom for us in this—the ability to chart our own course." This mindset, Robin adds, "better positions BNY to capitalize on megatrends in the industry, finding opportunities to fill gaps in the market

to show up differently for clients, and preparing employees for the future of work. That future is already here and, while many describe it in terms of technology, it is still inescapably human. And that is why culture is at the top of our agenda."

At Jeff Sprecher's ICE, and at BNY under Robin Vince, employees likely feel safe and empowered. They still need to have the 5Qs and social capital to advance; however, their employers provide them leverage, rather than holding them back.

One reason I wrote *Greatness Code* is to help people who are not working in positive leadership environments. I hope that every CEO and leader thinks very hard about the environment they create and keeps their eye on servant leadership, which, in my definition, means helping everyone who works in the organization achieve their Greatness Objectives.

ACG

Alan C. Guarino
4000 Ponce De Leon Blvd., Suite 410,
Coral Gables, Florida
October 10, 2025

About the Author

Leaders confer with him. They hire him to help them execute their strategies. Most importantly, they trust him.

Alan C. Guarino is a graduate of the U.S. Military Academy at West Point, His father immigrated to the United States in the 1920s, and then left school after the eighth grade. Alan was raised by working-class parents to value service, and strive to achieve. His Father eventually rose through the ranks in the construction industry and was highly respected. Like many Baby Boomers, he has lived the American Dream—rising from humble beginnings to become a trusted advisor to global leaders.

After attaining the rank of Captain in the U.S. Army and commanding a combat arms company in the Second Squadron, Sixth Cavalry, Alan began his Wall Street career at The Bank of New York. He was then hired into the recruiting industry by a regional firm in upstate New York. Then at age 33, he launched and bootstrapped a recruiting and consulting firm, ran it for a decade, and sold it to Adecco, a $30 billion global staffing company at the time. Today, he serves as Vice Chairman of Korn Ferry, the world's top-ranked leadership and talent consulting firm.

Over the course of his career, Alan has advised and recruited hundreds of top executives—guiding careers, transforming boards, and helping organizations around the world execute their strategies. His work, along with his colleagues, includes CEO search projects to find a CEO for E*TRADE during the global financial crisis; the CEO for the Wounded Warrior Project (WWP), placing General Michael Linnington, and President of the Federal Reserve Bank of Philadelphia, just to name a few.

Alan also served on the board of Chefs' Warehouse during its major post-IPO expansion, helping scale the company from $300 million to nearly $4 billion in annual revenue, with operations extending from the United States to Dubai.

He has counseled leaders across sectors—corporate, nonprofit, government, and education—and is a sought-after confidant by sovereign wealth funds, family offices, and global CEOs alike. He is an expert on the nuanced differences between Baby Boomers, Gen X, and Millennials in the context of their aspirations and their competencies, traits, and drivers, which are foundational to their career and life journeys.

Drawing on decades of insight observing human performance, Alan distilled the core elements of success into a powerful framework he shares in *Greatness Code*. Leaders trust him—not just for what he knows, but for how he helps them win.

Introduction

> Success is not final; failure is not fatal; it is the courage to continue that counts.
>
> —Winston Churchill

An individual's greatness is self-defined. For each of us—whether a plumber, professor, day-care provider, dancer, line cook, salesperson, stay-at-home parent, or top-level executive—the definition of success and the journey to achieve it is different. A *Greatness Objective* is personal.

Some people measure their success in dollars and cents; others set the bar based on a certain level of notoriety or recognition. Still others measure their value on selfless contributions to society, family devotion, or something else entirely. Regardless of the parameters, anyone who achieves their own greatness gets there by building on five critical qualities. I call them the **5Qs**:

- Persistence
- Stamina
- Courage
- Resilience
- Passion

These five developable qualities, plus an individual's *social capital* create the formula for greatness. Social capital refers to the network of people who support, guide and stand behind you; who, give you thoughtful, hard messages when needed, and mentor you. The 5Qs aren't flashy qualities; they're not something people instantly see or admire. But over time, they're unmistakable. The person who sticks with a project, keeps learning, and picks themselves up after a fall eventually stands out.

Most importantly, a personally defined goal of greatness is achievable for almost anyone with the right tools. In these pages, I'll provide those tools along with scientific research and real-life examples that help show how the formula can work for you.

If that sounds a bit too simple, consider that as a leadership practitioner—from my days as a cadet at the U.S. Military Academy at West Point to decades as a leader and as an advisor to many leaders—I've watched thousands of careers unfold and forge ahead, or derail and fail miserably. I know what works and what doesn't, and how individuals can strengthen each of the 5Qs as well as create the social capital network they need to optimize the greatness formula. Almost anyone can achieve their own *Greatness Objective*, whatever, wherever, and however different from the norm that goal might be. There are no set parameters and no right or wrong answers when it comes to personal Greatness Objectives.

When our children were young, my family traveled each year to Appalachia—specifically, Harlan, Kentucky—as a part of a Capuchin Franciscan mission project. Each mission lasted nine days, mostly spent repairing residents' homes, offering a children's bible school, and providing clothing in extremely rural and impoverished areas.

At the time, I was a consultant to firms on Wall Street and accustomed to working with people who often measured their successes in prestige and dollars and cents. When I returned from a mission trip, people I worked with often asked me, "How bad was it?"

My typical response surprised many: "I received more than I gave." I truly meant it. Typically, the missions meant we worked hard doing manual labor during the days and sleeping on a gym floor at the local Catholic church at night. But the work we did made a real difference for the people we helped. Most importantly, I told my colleagues, I know more happy people in Appalachia than on Wall Street.

Only a 10-hour drive southwest of New York City, this part of Appalachia was a world away. Few people had jobs. Sadly, a segment of the population struggled with drug addiction. Yet, most people were satisfied with their way of life, and there was an incredible sense of community that extended beyond just family. Basically, they had *faith, shelter, food, water, family, and friends*. If they measured success at all, they measured it against those metrics. This was their personal measure of greatness, and money was rarely part of it.

Watching a video or reading about Appalachia doesn't paint the real picture of sitting on a picnic table on a mountain, talking to a man raising his family there, and learning what was truly important to him. On one mission trip during a lunch break, while the teen volunteers in my crew were eating, the man whose home we were fixing walked with me across a couple of acres of the mountain he called home. It was dense with incredible hard-wood trees. His wife's family had owned this land for decades. That morning, when I met the man, he was pulling a small red wagon up the road from his brother-in-law's house. The wagon was filled with about 10 one-gallon jugs of drinking water. He told me his well pump wasn't working, so each morning he would go to his brother-in-law's house to get water for the day. This was in 2001.

After quickly scanning the woods during our lunchtime walk and knowing they owned hundreds of acres, I told him that his family likely had millions of dollars in timber at their disposal. I'm not a logging expert, but I have invested in timberland and understand its value. I asked the man why they didn't have a logging program that could provide family members some regular income. It would be good forest management and provide the family financial stability.

The man stopped and looked at me. "We would never do that," he said. "And besides, what would we do with the money?" This was a man, who with his wife and three children, lived in a single-wide trailer with three cramped bedrooms, a broken deck, and a leaky roof, not to mention no potable running water.

"Well, for one thing, you could buy a new well-pump," I replied.

"I really don't need one," he said, "since I can get water from my brother-in-law every day."

I thought for a moment. He was right. *He* did not need a well pump. I was the one who needed *him* to have the well pump. That's when I finally got it. At last, I understood that success takes many forms beyond wealth and status. It's a choice we all make that determines our quest for success—our *Greatness Objective*.

The Appalachia story is long, but telling, and one we can all take to heart in terms of finding our own Greatness Objectives. What is your career objective? What is greatness or success for you? Do you know why you are working? I assume you likely know how many *well-pumps*, if any, you want to have. I assume you know how the important metrics like faith, shelter, food, water, family, and friends matter to you.

No matter who you are, what your generation—Boomers to Gen X, Y, or Z—in these pages, you'll learn how and why answering those questions matters in any quest for success, however you define it. You'll better understand why the *5Qs*—essential qualities shared by successful people—matter. You'll learn the importance of social capital and how to build it as well as see how it has evolved among new generations and as our digital landscape.

After spending more than three decades learning and understanding leadership, I'm well-equipped to provide readers a solid blueprint for greatness. My studies began first as a student at West Point, then commanding a combat arms company in the Army, followed by a stint on Wall Street before turning to the recruiting and leadership consulting industry; eventually starting my own consulting and recruiting business. After the business was sold to Adecco, a $30-billion global staffing company at the time, I remained with Adecco for four years and eventually joined Korn Ferry (NYSE: KFY). Korn Ferry, where I am currently Vice Chairman, is regularly ranked number one in the industry by *Forbes* magazine.

Over the years, I've helped recruit hundreds of executives, including for some of the world's leading Fortune 500 companies. I know what makes great employees and great leaders, what doesn't, and why. From those experiences, the *Greatness Code* formula for success has evolved.

The book is divided into four sections that break down and detail what it takes to build, maximize, and sustain personal success from early in a career to mid-career and peak career. Then, I outline how to continue to achieve and maintain chosen objectives for success following your career peak. Included, you will find practical exercises to help guide, explain, and encourage your own success as well as provide a workable, understandable framework for achievement as you strive to reach your greatness objective.

Introduction xxiii

Nothing is static in life, the 5Qs and social capital included. Though the basic principles remain the same, each evolves in response to societal changes, new challenges, and different opportunities. The advent of digitization, the globalization of labor markets, artificial intelligence and the shifting nature of work, all have redefined what it means to persevere artificial intelligence and connect. Different generations identify greatness differently, too.

So, if you're ready to pursue your own greatness, turn the page and let's get started.

ACG

Alan C. Guarino
July 23, 2025
New York, NY

Portions of this text were drafted with assistance from ChatGPT by Open ai. This AI tool helped with drafting and editing, research, and educational content to organize my ideas, suggest alternative phrasing for various concepts, and improve clarity and conciseness throughout the writing process. All AI-generated content was carefully reviewed, edited, and approved. The final analysis, conclusions, and interpretations represent my views and expertise.

GREATNESS CODE

PART 1

Early Stage: Laying the Foundations

1 | Early Challenges Will Build the Right Muscles

> Nothing in the world is worth having or worth doing unless it means effort, pain, difficulty.
> —Theodore Roosevelt

Each of us defines success—our personal Greatness Objective—differently. For some, it's about generating a certain amount of cash; others rely on a level of recognition, notoriety, family, friends, devotion, or amount of free time. Indeed, during our lives we have parallel Greatness Objectives. For some, while striving for career success, they are also striving to be great parents, or community leaders, or musicians, or whatever. Regardless of someone's objectives, my formula works. The journey to achieve any *Greatness Objective* requires five crucial qualities—the 5Qs:

1. Persistence
2. Stamina

3. Courage
4. Resilience
5. Passion

When a person combines these five developable qualities with social capital, the result is a formula for personal greatness. Social capital is the network of people who support, guide, and stand behind you; who give you thoughtful, hard messages when needed, and open doors for you along your journey. Without this network you can only get so far.

The 5Qs aren't flashy qualities, but practiced over time, they're unmistakable. Think about the fellow worker who always sticks with a project, constantly learns new things, and never fails to get back up after being knocked down.

Grit: A Commonality

Almost anyone can achieve their own Greatness Objective, whatever it is, wherever they are, and however different from the norm that goal might be. There are no set parameters, no right or wrong answers, and no single map for the journey.

A commonality upfront, though, is grit. The journey to success begins with the courage and resolve to succeed, no matter the challenges. Over time, applying grit to your work can bring a sense of accomplishment that no single success can match. Grit enables you to build a foundation through resilience, adaptability, and self-confidence. It teaches you to trust in your own ability to handle whatever comes your way, no matter how daunting. In a world that values quick wins and visible achievements, people with grit stand out because they are invested in the journey, not just the destination.

The Duckworth Equation

In the late 1990s, psychologist Angela Duckworth wanted to understand why some people persist and others give up. At the time, Duckworth was a seventh-grade math teacher in New York City, watching her students struggle with fractions and algebra. Many of us have experienced that same thing. For some, it ends up a rite of passage we eventually survive. To others, though, those numbers represent an insurmountable challenge.

Duckworth noticed the same thing, and that those who thrived in her classroom weren't necessarily the *smart* kids. Instead, those who eventually mastered fractions and algebra didn't back down from the tough problems, continually erased and rewrote, asked questions, and willingly owned up to the challenges. In those successes, Duckworth identified the foundation of a unique driver, what she later labeled *grit*.

Grit, Duckworth discovered, wasn't just about endurance. It was, she later wrote in her bestseller, *Grit: The Power of Passion and Perseverance* (2018), a person's attitude toward long-term goals that drives a commitment to something meaningful. That something "meaningful" is what I call an individual's *Greatness Objective*.

Whatever the chosen moniker, the bottom line is that talent alone can't compete against someone willing to work tirelessly with an eye toward a *Greatness Objective* often miles away.

An Early-Career Must

Grit remains crucial, especially for everyone early in their careers. It helps someone stay in the game despite rocky roads and distant payoffs. I describe it more granularly, beyond simply perseverance and passion, it is the 5Qs. The best part is that almost anyone can develop these qualities. Like strong muscles, you don't have to be born with them, but with practice, patience, and a willingness to push through discomfort, they grow strong.

Reshma Saujani: Stretch Goals, Career Pivots, and the Power of Building a Network

Imagine having an idea and then eventually reaching billions of people with it. Reshma Saujani did just that. She founded *Girls Who Code*, an organization dedicated to closing the gender gap in technology, and I spoke to her about it. Since its founding, Girls Who Code has made a significant impact, reaching over 14.6 billion people, and directly serving 700,000 girls. Across the United States, more than 6,000 Girls Who Code clubs have been launched to expand access to technology education for middle and high school girls.

Saujani's journey is one of resilience, bold career pivots, and a relentless commitment to empowering others. Her career didn't start in tech—nor did it follow a conventional path. Instead, it was marked by failures, reinventions, and the power of building a network that could support and amplify her impact.

Born to Indian immigrant parents who fled Uganda, Saujani grew up with the deeply ingrained values of education and hard work. She pursued a legal career, earning degrees from the University of Illinois, Harvard's Kennedy School, and Yale Law School. Like many ambitious professionals, she had a clear vision of success: She would become a lawyer, make an impact, and rise through the ranks. However, things didn't go according to plan. After graduating from Yale, she struggled to secure a legal job in the wake of the 2008 financial crisis. Rejections piled up, and she found herself questioning everything she had worked toward. But instead of accepting defeat, she decided to take a risk by pivoting—and setting herself on a completely new path.

Saujani had always been drawn to public service, and in 2010, she made a bold decision: She ran for U.S. Congress in New York's 14th district, challenging a long-time incumbent. It was an uphill battle. She had no prior political experience, no political family connections, and was up against an entrenched system. She poured everything into the race, working tirelessly, knocking on thousands of doors, and speaking about the issues that mattered to her.

Despite her passion, she lost. The defeat had to be painful. Public failure at such a large scale is often enough to deter even the most determined individuals. But for Saujani, it became the catalyst for reinvention. She had put herself in the arena, built a network of supporters, and learned lessons that would shape her next move. While campaigning, during visits to local schools, she noticed something striking: a stark gender divide in computer science classrooms. This observation ultimately led her to establish Girls Who Code in 2012. Pursuing this was a big stretch.

Through advocacy, programs, and community-driven initiatives, Girls Who Code continues working toward closing the gender gap in the technology sector. The organization has set an ambitious goal of achieving gender parity in entry-level tech jobs by 2030.

With no background in tech, she was an unlikely leader for such an initiative. But what she lacked in technical expertise, she made up for in vision, persistence, and an ability to rally the right people to the cause.

Saujani understood that she couldn't do it alone. She leveraged every connection she had—from politicians she met on the campaign trail to business leaders, educators, and Silicon Valley executives—to build support for Girls Who Code. She convinced major companies like Google, Microsoft, and Facebook to invest in the organization, helping it scale from a small pilot program to a national movement that has now reached hundreds of thousands of girls.

Her ability to build and nurture a powerful social network was critical to Girls Who Code's success. She didn't just focus on funding—she built relationships creating social capital that would provide mentorship opportunities for young girls, change hiring practices in tech companies, and create a community that would uplift and support women in the industry.

Despite the success of Girls Who Code, Saujani faced challenges that tested her resilience. As the organization grew, so did the scrutiny. Leading a nonprofit at a national scale meant navigating internal politics, public expectations, and the constant pressure to do more with limited resources.

Saujani led the organization as CEO for nine years. In 2019, she stepped away to focus on new initiatives. For many, leaving an organization they built from the ground up can spur an identity crisis, but Saujani saw it as another evolution—a chance to pivot again, to apply her skills in a new way.

After stepping away from *Girls Who Code*, Saujani turned her attention to women in the workforce, particularly how the COVID-19 pandemic disproportionately affected working mothers. In 2021, she launched the Marshall Plan for Moms, advocating for paid parental leave, affordable childcare, and policies that support working families. Once again, she used her network—activists, corporate leaders, and policymakers—to bring attention to an issue that had long been overlooked.

In 2022, Saujani formalized this initiative by founding the Moms First organization (initially known by the same name as the campaign), which seeks to mobilize public and private sector support to better support mothers. She has also continued to write and speak on gender equity, releasing her book *Pay Up: The Future of Women and Work (and Why It's Different Than You Think)* in 2022. The book offers a bold critique of modern workplace culture and proposes actionable solutions for employers and policymakers. The organization's events are powerful. The Moms First Summit in May of 2024, highlighted some of the organization's initiatives, noting "They laid out real solutions to how we win the fights for paid leave, affordable child care, and equal pay—the structural supports moms need to thrive."

Through advocacy, writing, and coalition-building, Saujani has become a leading voice for systemic change, expanding her influence beyond tech and education to champion a future of work that truly values women and caregivers. Her advocacy has led to major companies rethinking their workplace policies and has influenced the national conversation on gender equity in the workplace. Just as she did with Girls Who Code, Saujani identified a systemic issue, built a movement, and rallied people around a cause.

I asked her what advice should would give to others who are striving to reach a Greatness Objective. She said, "If you want to live a great life, don't chase perfection. Chase purpose. Be brave enough to fail. Be stubborn enough to try again. And build a community strong enough to carry you through."

Saujani's journey exemplifies grit in action—the ability to embrace failure, pivot when necessary, and build networks that amplify one's impact. Her story offers key takeaways for anyone looking to build a meaningful career.

Lessons from Reshma Saujani's Career

- Failure is not the end, but the beginning. Losing a political race could have discouraged Saujani from pursuing leadership, but instead, it opened the door to something even more impactful.
- Career pivots require courage. Moving from law to politics, then to tech and advocacy, Saujani continually reinvented herself, proving that adaptability is key to long-term success.
- Your social-capital network is a critical asset. By forging strong relationships, she was able to scale Girls Who Code and advocate effectively for policy change.
- Resilience means pushing through rejection. From job rejections to election losses, she refused to let setbacks define her.

Saujani has changed the landscape for young women in tech and working mothers across the country. She has shown that success is not about following a linear path; it's about being courageous enough to pivot, persistent enough to push through obstacles, and adept enough to build a network that supports your vision.

Her story is a testament to the power of the 5Qs and social capital, turning setbacks into stepping stones. Whether you're an aspiring entrepreneur, an apprentice in the building trades, a professional facing career uncertainty, or someone simply seeking to make an impact, Saujani's journey offers a blueprint for success in a fast-paced, complex, global world.

My Material Stretch Goals Evolved to Something More

I grew up in Danbury, Connecticut, the child of working-class parents. My father was an Italian immigrant who came to America as a child in the 1920s. He left school after eighth grade—a relatively common practice at the time. My parents were smart, but lacked educational opportunities. Like so many others, they made their way in blue- and gray-collar jobs. My neighbors were plumbers and truck drivers, great people from The Greatest Generation.

As a child, if I wanted us to buy something, my dad often said, "Sorry, we can't afford that, but maybe someday you will be able to buy things like that by going to school and working hard." My parents, like so many others of their generation, required us to strive for academic credentials as the keys to career success.

And so I did. I graduated from West Point with a bachelor of science degree, and then a few years later earned an MBA while serving as an officer in the U.S. Army. After leaving the Army at age 27, I was working at The Bank of New York on Wall Street and quickly learned it was untenable with a 4-hour daily commute. So rather than relocate, I looked for a job closer to home. I joined Career Directions, a regional staffing company near my home and learned the recruiting business. We were not making big money, yet my career-related stretch goal focused on money. Remembering my childhood when I wanted things we couldn't afford, I over-indexed on making money. I said to my wife, "I'll have a Rolex watch by the time I'm 30 and I'll be a millionaire by the time I'm 35." At the time I was young and it made sense. Looking back, it's embarrassing to admit those goals. But, in the 1980s, financial success was a big deal, especially where I grew up.

When I turned 30, somehow my wife still found a way to buy me a Rolex for my birthday. It was a pre-owned watch, but it was a Rolex, just the same. With the gift, her note said, "I wanted you to keep the first promise, so you'd be sure to keep the second!" Three years later, we started our company.

We were fortunate after a decade to sell our company to Adecco, the largest staffing company in the world at the time, with about $30 billion in annual revenue. Our company was successful, but in our industry, we were still a boutique firm. The *big leagues* in the industry were the five major firms that had pioneered the industry. One of those firms was Korn Ferry. In 2007, I was fortunate to be hired by them. I went there for one primary reason—my stretch goal. I set that goal because I wanted to see if I could excel in the big leagues.

My goal was not just to survive as a partner, but to achieve industry recognition. I wanted to be selected to work with companies and solve key executive talent challenges that could impact the world. When you help put a new CEO into a company, you not only change that person's life; you change the lives of arguably thousands of people, from the company's employees to its customers, suppliers, and shareholders. At the time, I focused on fintech, then an emerging market within financial services.

What right did I have to think I could play at this level? Korn Ferry was the top executive search firm in the world. I probably didn't have any right—but I had a stretch goal to cap off my career and achieve my *Greatness Objective* as I defined it.

Ideally, the greatness you strive for is defined by you. When you get there it's likely you will be the only one who knows. During my first five years at the firm, I threw myself at the job, met with lots of rejection pursuing clients, gained almost 50 pounds, and eventually ended up with cardiac stents from the stress and lack of time at the gym. (Too often, I opted to meet with clients instead of hopping on a treadmill.)

Success at work was everything. It probably almost killed me. During the period, one of my colleagues asked me what kept me pushing ahead. I told him the answer was simple. I was scared to death; I was afraid to fall short. When I woke up each morning, I felt like a pack of dogs was chasing me, and I couldn't slow down. This was self-imposed. Slowing down wasn't an option.

Finally in 2013, after six years with the company, Korn Ferry appointed me vice chairman. That satisfied my professional stretch goal in my industry.

My next stretch goal was personal—to lose 50 pounds. I finally did it; but it took another seven years. The Greatness Code fundamentals apply in all aspects of your life, both personal and professional.

After 2013, I pivoted my focus to mentoring and innovation rather than just new stretch goals. I sought out members of the firm who wanted to expand their business-development skills. I enjoyed challenging them to think bigger, and to avoid putting limits on what they thought was possible.

Additionally, I put more focus into lifelong learning. I wanted to continually find new and better ways to deliver solutions for clients. This led me to study ways to optimize human capital within organizations. That came from the *passion* part of the 5Qs. Plenty of my clients probably want to tell me, "Will you shut up already." They're tired of hearing me say that we are in the talent-age, and that the talent agenda will determine an organization's success far more than any investment in technology. But that's the truth, even in the age of artificial intelligence.

How You Can Set Effective Stretch Goals

Setting a stretch goal requires a balance between ambition and realism. The goal should feel challenging enough to push you out of your comfort zone, but also attainable enough that you believe it's possible with the right effort.

And don't be afraid of failure. Instead, embrace it as a learning opportunity that's crucial to build the 5Qs. My company, Korn Ferry, points out that people who see setbacks as opportunities to grow, are more likely to persist and ultimately succeed. That perspective transforms failure from a deterrent into a valuable component of the learning process.

How to set a Stretch Goal

- **Identify a goal with meaning.** Start with something that genuinely excites you, that feels like it could have a lasting impact on your personal or professional growth. A good stretch goal is tied to a purpose that motivates you.

(continued)

> *(continued)*
> - **Break the goal into milestones.** A stretch goal can feel overwhelming if you try to tackle it all at once. Break it down into smaller manageable, measurable milestones that provide a way for regular wins to celebrate along the way.
> - **Visualize the outcome.** Visualization is a powerful tool. Take time to picture your achievement of the goal. Imagine the process and the success. Visualization helps to build emotional commitment and resilience.
> - **Commit to the process, not just the outcome, and tell others about it.** Focus on daily actions that will lead to the goal. Commit to showing up every day and putting in the work, even when progress feels slow. Celebrate the small wins along the way to stay energized. This commitment to the process is what sustains us. Telling others makes you more accountable. Writing it down helps you commit, too.
> - **Fail forward; embrace setbacks as growth opportunities.** If you ask most people to describe failure, they probably will talk about the sting of rejection, embarrassment, and feeling you're not good enough. But for those who embody the 5Qs, failure looks different. In their eyes, it's an opportunity—a stepping stone to the next iteration of their success story. And in this way, gritty people don't just bounce back from failure. They fail forward.

Korn Ferry research underscores the importance of the 5Qs in achieving sustained success, setting stretch goals, seeing failures as learning opportunities, and engaging in daily practices that build resilience. All that combined helps individuals cultivate the resilience, persistence, courage, stamina, and passion necessary to reach their long-term greatness objectives.

It's Not Always about the Corporate Workplace

These important qualities, approaches, and strategies aren't just mantras for corporate professionals. They apply to all of us, whatever direction our lives take. How to reframe failures, for example, is something everyone needs to learn.

Learn From Dean Dillon—Listen to the Music

In corporate terms, if major country music performers are the CEOs of their respective divisions, then Dean Dillon is the CPO (chief product officer). You ask, "Who the hell is Dean Dillon?" Dillon began his career in the early 1970s. In 1973, right out of high school, he hitchhiked to Nashville and pounded on record labels' doors trying to get a job. He initially tried his hand as a performer and songwriter. While facing early struggles, including sleeping in a coal bin under a building in Nashville and working odd jobs, he eventually abandoned his performing career to focus solely on songwriting, where he found his true calling.

Dean *failed forward* by shifting full time into song writing and abandoning his dream of being a performer. He told the record company "put a fork in it; I'm done. I just wanna' write songs from now on." However, as a songwriter he was still not an overnight success. Two years before Dean went to Nashville, music legend Merle Haggard told him that it would take him every bit of seven years of rejection to get to the point where he might be writing music that Nashville would be interested in. How was he supposed to survive if he had had no money and had no shot at success for that many years? And there was no guarantee he would make it at all. So, let's recap: He hitchhiked to Nashville with no money to pursue a career as a country music star; he was rejected repeatedly year after year; he slept in a coal bin; yet he persisted. It would have been far easier to find some other less ambitious career and walk away.

Along his journey, Dillon collected some key people in his social-capital network including Hank Cochran who took him under his wing. It was also great performers who loved his melodies and his lyrics. This made all the difference. Gary Stewart also seemed to be an important connection as Dillon worked on his songwriting style. Your social-capital network doesn't have to be expansive, but it has to be impactful.

Dillon's big break came in the very late 1970s when he finally began writing songs for major country artists. His first top 10 hit as a songwriter was "Lying in Love with You," co-written with Gary Stewart and performed by Jim Ed Brown and Helen Cornelius.

Early Stage: Laying the Foundations

I met Dillon when he was honored in Huntsville, Alabama, in 2024. He said that when he heard his song come over the radio for the first time, he was driving on the freeway. He pulled the car over and cried. He said it was amazing that a song he wrote was good enough to be played on the radio. In the 2017 TV documentary *Tennessee Whiskey: The Dean Dillon Story*, Dean explains that his first hit happened almost seven years to the day that Merle Haggard told him he had at least seven years of rejection before he might make it. This is a reminder that all we are exploring in this book about goals and ambition is rarely easy and likely takes time. In the early stage of a career, staying positive requires patience.

Dillon's journey to one of country music's most esteemed songwriters is a testament to social capital and the 5Qs. Despite challenges, he remained steadfast in his pursuit of a music career. At a time when the Nashville music scene had a particular image, Dillon was advised to cut his long hair to fit industry standards. Choosing authenticity over conformity, he retained his personal style, a decision that reflected his commitment to his true self.

How successful was his career? Many believe he is the best Nashville has ever seen. Notable hits include "Marina del Rey," "The Chair," "I've Come to Expect It from You," "Easy Come, Easy Go," and "The Best Day." There are many, many more. Dillon worked with many artists, contributing to the success of chart topping songs like "Tennessee Whiskey," which has been covered by numerous performers, including George Jones, David Allan Coe, and Chris Stapleton. This body of work likely represents tens of millions of records sold in his career.

To make his challenges greater, he also had to overcome addiction, which he was also able to conquer.

Failing forward is real. I told Dillon that in my own struggles I found lots of help from music. My friends and family will tell you it's the only music my truck radio knows how to play.

Country music is often about hardship and overcoming struggles. I've had my share, as have all of us. I credit Dean Dillon's melodies and lyrics for helping me through the hard times.

While writing this book, I have gotten to know Dean a bit. On top of all his accomplishments, it's important to also note that he's a really good guy.

Table 1.1   Embracing Failure

Strategy	Description
Analyze Failures Objectively	After a setback, first ask yourself, "How did I mess this up?" Don't dwell on negative emotions. Instead, break down what happened objectively. What specific actions or decisions led to the result? Which are attributable to *you* and which to others? This analysis can reveal insights that help you avoid similar pitfalls in the future.
Separate Yourself from the Outcome	Gritty individuals don't tie their self-worth to a single outcome. Remember that failure is part of the process, not a reflection of your value or potential. This mental separation makes it easier to bounce back.
Find the Silver Lining	Every failure, no matter how painful, has a silver lining. It could be a lesson, new direction, or opportunity for self-improvement. By focusing on what you've gained rather than what you've lost, you shift from a fixed mindset to a growth mindset.
Embrace a Growth Mindset	Embracing the *growth mindset*, a concept coined by psychologist Carol Dweck, can be transformational. Instead of seeing your abilities as fixed, recognize that each experience, including failure, contributes to your growth and skill development.

Failing forward is a skill, and like any skill, it takes practice to develop. Table 1.1 shows a few strategies for cultivating a healthy relationship with failure.

The Science Behind the 5Qs and a Warning for Parents Who Make Life Too Easy for Kids

The five qualities necessary for greatness—stamina, courage, resilience, passion, and persistence (SCRPP)—have been studied extensively by psychologists, neuroscientists, and educators who seek to understand how early development equips individuals to cope with adversity and maintain ambition. Table 1.2 summarizes a few of those insights and how they foster resilience and goal-directed behavior.

Table 1.2 Research Summarized

Topic	Key Research/Concept	Findings/Implications
Stress Inoculation Theory and Tolerance for Discomfort	Donald Meichenbaum	Exposure to moderate, manageable stress "inoculates" individuals against future stressors by teaching coping mechanisms.
Cumulative Adversity and Resilience	Seery, Holman, & Silver (2010)	Moderate levels of lifetime adversity lead to greater resilience and life satisfaction compared to low or high adversity.
Mastery Experiences and Resilience	Albert Bandura's Theory of Self-Efficacy	Success in challenging tasks enhances confidence and fosters the belief in one's ability to handle future challenges.
Executive Function Development	Diamond (2013)	Activities requiring sustained effort and delayed gratification strengthen the prefrontal cortex, promote resilience.
Moderate Stress and Emotional Growth	Ellis, Bianchi, Griskevicius, & Frankenhuis (2017)	Moderate stress exposure fine-tunes stress-response systems, enhances emotional regulation and adaptability.
Early Challenges and Grit Development	Angela Duckworth (2018)	Early structured challenges build perseverance foster long-term success and the ability to endure discomfort.

Neural Adaptation and the Brain's Reward System

Early development of the quality of persistence can, as science calls it, enhance neural plasticity. That's in part what helps someone adapt to new experiences and learn and acquire new skills (Knudsen, 2004). When children practice perseverance through activities like problem-solving or learning a musical instrument, it reinforces the neural pathways associated with goal-directed behavior, making it easier to persist in the face of future challenges.

Dopamine and Sustaining Effort

Scientific research shows overcoming challenges actually can trigger the body to release dopamine—the feel-good hormone. That creates a positive feedback loop in the brain's reward system, conditioning someone to associate effort with potential rewards. In simple terms, that means our brains actually work to help us sustain long-term ambition and persistence.

Psychological Resilience Through Repeated Exposure to Challenges

Science also tells us that our exposure at a young age to moderate levels of stress can help build our tolerance for discomfort. The result is greater emotional and psychological resilience.

Analysis by Seery et al. (2010) found that individuals who experienced manageable adversity earlier in life were better equipped to handle stress and adversity later, compared to those with either no adversity or excessive hardship. Carol Dweck's groundbreaking work on the growth mindset (Dweck, 2006) found that children who believe their abilities can be developed through effort are more likely to persist through setbacks, demonstrating higher levels of grit.

Long-Term Impact on Ambition

Eskreis-Winkler et al. (2014) also found that an individual's level of grit predicted higher retention and performance in a variety of high-stress environments. Their study included a sampling from military training to corporate jobs. These findings suggest that early experiences of grit help individuals build the capacity for sustained effort and goal achievement.

Emotional Regulation and Stress Management

The prefrontal cortex, responsible for decision-making and impulse control, is particularly malleable during childhood. Research by Diamond (2013) indicates that activities that require sustained attention and self-regulation—hallmarks of grit—strengthen this brain region and enhance an individual's ability to manage stress and focus on long-term goals.

Studies on cortisol levels, like those by Miller et al. (2007), suggest that individuals with higher resilience—often cultivated through early experiences of grit—exhibit more stable stress hormone levels. This physiological stability makes them less prone to being overwhelmed by adversity.

Social and Behavioral Reinforcement

Social learning theory, as outlined by Bandura (1977), posits that children model behaviors they observe in others. Exposure to role models who demonstrate grit, like parents or mentors, provides children with a behavioral blueprint to handle challenges and persist through difficulties.

Self-Awareness and Agility Matter

When it comes to achieving career success and one's Greatness Objective, while the research is important, understanding that individual traits don't exist in isolation is key. Instead, the various qualities interplay with each other.

For example, consider learning agility. That's the ability to know what to do when you don't know what to do. It's an individual's capacity to learn from experience, adapt to new situations, and apply lessons to solve novel challenges, according to Korn Ferry.

Learning agility also explains how the Peter Principle often happens. That's a management principle coined by author Laurence J. Peter that describes the person who is over-promoted based on past performance, not not future potential, and eventually fails. That person may have been a high performer in a previous job, but they lack the learning agility to achieve at the next level.

Learning agility can be measured using special psychometric assessments. But instead, companies often promote people solely based on managerial reviews and that's not enough. Korn Ferry identifies five key dimensions to learning agility—self-awareness, mental agility, people agility, change agility, and results agility. These dimensions enable individuals to adapt quickly in a constantly changing work environment and complement grit by ensuring that persistent efforts are directed toward relevant and impactful goals.

Looking more closely:

- Self-awareness enables an individual to know their limits. Pursuing advancement too early or beyond one's capacity can lead to career ruin.
- Mental agility allows professionals to analyze complex problems and find innovative solutions.
- People agility helps someone collaborate effectively with diverse teams, and build a social capital network.
- Learning agility, when paired with grit's focus on perseverance, ensures that individuals not only stay the course but also adjust their strategies when necessary to achieve success.

A Word about Generational Differences (or Not)

As we examine modern careers, it's clear that the narrative surrounding success has shifted. Baby Boomers, born into an era marked by economic expansion and relative stability, are often lauded for their work ethic, resilience, and stamina. This generation has largely been rewarded for its dedication, achieving financial security and professional recognition. But for the generations that followed—the Gen Xers, Millennials (Gen Y), and Gen Z—this has proven to be more elusive, shaped by economic volatility, technological disruption, and cultural shifts. These younger cohorts have not only faced a different set of challenges but have also been subjected to harsher judgments, often broadly described as less industrious or committed than their predecessors.

Misunderstood or Not?

This differences between generations raises a compelling question: Have the generations following the Baby Boomers truly lacked the 5Qs and social capital, or have they simply been misunderstood? While it's true that Millennials and Gen Z have encountered systemic barriers to financial success—rising student debt, stagnant wages, high housing costs, high taxes, and diminished access to traditional wealth-building opportunities—it is equally true that these same generations are, admirably reshaping the definition of success.

By leveraging their unique strengths, including adaptability, creativity, and a commitment to collective progress, they are poised to bring about advancements that will redefine the parameters of achievement for the future. I suspect it will not be as focused on a financial achievement scorecard, but then isn't that what a Greatness Objective is all about. It's personal.

5Qs and Social Capital: From Cave People to Today

The 5Qs and social capital always have been integral to human progress. Consider early explorers who braved uncharted seas or the social capital of community-based economies where trade and trust formed the bedrock of prosperity. These qualities were indispensable in ancient societies, where survival often depended on a delicate balance of individual tenacity and collaborative effort.

Fast-forward to the Industrial Revolution, a period that demanded extraordinary qualities from laborers who endured grueling factory conditions and social capital from entrepreneurs building vast networks to fuel economic expansion. The post-World War II era, which gave rise to the Baby Boomer generation, was similarly defined by these traits. Hard work, coupled with robust social networks and government policies that supported upward mobility, enabled this generation to achieve significant milestones in education, homeownership, and career advancement. Notably, they worked in corporate environments that were far more forgiving than today's. Pace, complexity, and globalization have made corporate life brutal compared with corporate life of the 1970s, '80s, '90s, and early 2000s.

The 5Qs and social capital are not static. They evolve in response to societal changes and adapt to new challenges and opportunities. For the generations that followed the Boomers, the contexts in which these qualities operate have changed dramatically. The advent of the digital age, artificial intelligence, the globalization of labor markets, and the shifting nature of work have redefined what it means to persevere and connect.

Baby Boomers, the Standard-Bearers of Grit

While clearly not rivaling the grit of the Greatest Generation (e.g., no Great Depression and no world wars to fight), the Baby Boomer generation has been heralded as the epitome of the 5Q's. Born in decades following World War II, they entered a world characterized by rapid economic growth and the promise of the American Dream. For many Boomers, success was a straightforward equation: work hard, climb the corporate ladder, and reap the rewards of financial stability and social respectability. Many companies offered a job for life if you wanted it, as long as you at least achieved minimum standards. Their efforts were often met with tangible outcomes—steady jobs, pensions, and a sense of security that fostered optimism and a feeling of safety. This applied to others such as those in the trades.

But this narrative, while compelling, oversimplifies the context in which Boomers operated. Their grit was undoubtedly real, but it was also supported by systemic advantages. The post-war era provided unprecedented access to affordable education, strong unions, and government-backed loans for housing. Social capital thrived in an environment where communities were more interconnected, face-to-face relationship building was the norm, and trust in institutions remained relatively high. People had time to cultivate real connections in a relatively slow-paced environment.

I started work in the 1980s, and still remember the first time an executive's assistant asked if I'd like to schedule a call with him. It was actually a new concept. Scheduling a call? Prior to this new phenomenon, you called someone and they often answered the phone, or you left them a message on their answering machine. They often called back before the end of the day. A faster pace brought about scheduled phone calls on packed calendars. By the late 1990s, it started to feel like the norm. Today, we fully expect we will need to schedule a call to speak to someone. So, as we think about the work environment that evolved as Baby Boomers progressed, remember this simple example. The pace of work became more relentless.

The Generational Shift from Boomers to Millennials and Beyond

As the Baby Boomers aged and the world transformed, the path to success grew more complex. Gen X, Millennials (Gen Y), and Gen Z inherited a landscape marked by rapid pace, globalization, complexity, technological disruption, and economic uncertainty. For these generations, the relationship between grit and reward has been less linear, leading to perceptions of their efforts as less substantial or impactful. I contend that the 5Q's and social capital are now even more important for them; they face a tougher climb. Additionally, social capital is a strong differentiator for them. Remote work and the orientation toward digital and social media reduce human connection. So those who take the time to get out and meet people in person will make stronger bonds.

Take Millennials. This generation entered the workforce during the Great Recession, a time when traditional markers of success—homeownership, stable employment, and wealth accumulation—became harder to achieve. Despite these challenges, Millennials have demonstrated remarkable resilience, adapting to gig economies, embracing lifelong learning, and building careers in an era of unprecedented change. Their grit manifests not in the conventional sense of climbing a corporate ladder but in their ability to pivot, innovate, and persevere in the face of systemic barriers.

Social capital, too, has taken on new dimensions. Younger generations have mastered the art of digital networking, and built relationships and influence through platforms that transcend geographical and social boundaries. While their networks may look different from their predecessors', they are no less powerful. In fact, the collaborative ethos of Millennials and Gen Z, coupled with their commitment to diversity and inclusion, has expanded the very definition of social capital to encompass global and intersectional communities. However, I do want to reinforce that in-person connection is and added multiplier.

Unfair Judgments and Misunderstandings

Despite their accomplishments, Millennials (born 1981–1996) and Gen Z (born 1996–2010) have often been criticized as entitled, lazy, or unwilling to work hard. (The next cohort, Gen Alpha was born 2010 through the mid-2020s, so they aren't yet in the workforce.) These stereotypes ignore the structural challenges these generations face, as well as the ways in which they are redefining success. Unlike the Baby Boomers (born 1946–1964), who benefited from a relatively stable economic and social environment, younger generations have had to navigate a world in flux. Their grit is not less than that of their predecessors—it is simply different, shaped by the demands of a rapidly evolving world. By the way, if you do the research, you can find newspaper clippings back to the late 1800s with similar criticisms that cite the *current* generation "doesn't want to work" and that the future in that context looks bleak.

Millennials have been labeled job hoppers, a trait often interpreted as a lack of loyalty or perseverance. Yet, this tendency reflects their adaptability and willingness to seek opportunities in a volatile job market. It also stems from the fact that companies are far more likely to eliminate jobs than they were during the early careers of the Baby Boomers.

Loyalty cuts both ways. Workers don't see the safety that was apparent in the 1980s and 1990s, so they hop if an opportunity avails itself. Similarly, Gen Z's emphasis on work-life balance and mental health is sometimes viewed as a lack of commitment. In reality, it represents a shift toward sustainable success, where well-being is prioritized alongside career achievement. Again, placing less emphasis on the financial scorecard as the yardstick of success.

A Legacy of Grit and Connection

The story of grit and social capital is not confined to any one generation. It is a universal narrative, woven through the fabric of human history. While the challenges and opportunities of each era differ, the qualities that drive success remain constant.

For Baby Boomers, grit and social capital took the form of hard work and community engagement within a stable and safe system. For Millennials and Gen Z, these qualities are expressed through adaptability, innovation, a realistic assessment of what advancement may actually be attainable, and a commitment to globalism.

Today's Early Career Cohort

From a timing perspective, the lines between generational cohorts may blur and overlap. However, most Millennials and Gen Zers fall into the early-career category right now. Elder Millennials, now in their 40s, may be in the mid-career stage or ending their early careers. Career peaks typically start in a person's late 40s to late 50s.

Todays Early Career Cohort. Millennials and Gen Z

> **Research-Based Generalizations: Millennials**
>
> The following are some generalizations from various research sources about Millennials (Gen Y):
>
> - **Impatience for rapid career growth:** Millennials expect quick advancement in their careers due to their upbringing during rapid technological advancements. When growth opportunities are slow, they often feel disengaged or dissatisfied. (See Papadatou, 2019.)
>
> *(continued)*

(continued)

- **Financial challenges:** Millennials are burdened with significant student debt and high living costs, which can limit their ability to take risks, like pursuit of entrepreneurial ventures or further education. (See Krueger, 2023.)
- **Negative stereotypes:** Common perceptions of Millennials as entitled or job-hoppers can affect employer trust, requiring Millennials to go above and beyond to demonstrate commitment and reliability. (See Sananka et al., 2023.)
- **Burnout from overcommitment:** Millennials strive for a strong work-life balance but often overcommit to responsibilities, leading to exhaustion and job dissatisfaction. (See Talker Research, 2025.)
- **Navigating an evolving job market:** Millennials faced a challenging job market during the Great Recession, which often led to underemployment or delays in starting their ideal careers.
- **High expectations for purpose-driven work:** Like Millennials, they seek meaning and purpose in their work. However, this pursuit can result in frequent job changes that disrupt career stability. (See Deloitte, 2025, "2025 Gen Z and Millennial Survey," and Thomas, 2023.)
- **Struggles with workplace hierarchies:** Millennials tend to value flexibility and inclusivity, which can clash with traditional workplace structures, making it difficult for them to adapt to rigid hierarchies. (See Deloitte, 2023).
- **Emotional intelligence gaps:** A lack of emotional intelligence can lead to challenges in teamwork, conflict resolution, and leadership, stalling career growth. (See Winarni, 2023.)
- **Navigating job market saturation:** Millennials entered the workforce amid increasing competition, which often led to settling for roles below their skill level or experiencing extended periods of job searching.
- **Gender pay disparities:** Millennial women still face wage gaps, which can reduce job satisfaction and impede long-term financial stability. (See Fry and Aragão, 2025.)

> **Research-based Generalizations: Gen Z**
>
> The following are some research-based generalizations about Gen Z:
>
> - **Overreliance on technology:** As digital natives, Gen Z often excels in technology-driven roles but may lack interpersonal skills like networking and face-to-face communication. (See Segal, 2024.)
> - **Entrepreneurial risks:** Many in Gen Z embrace entrepreneurship, but lack strong financial foundations, high EQ, or risk mitigation strategies. Their ventures can fail quickly and lead to career instability. (See British Council Corporate Insights, 2023.)
> - **Demand for flexibility:** Gen Z prioritizes remote work and autonomy, which may limit opportunities in industries or roles that require strict office presence or hierarchical compliance. (See Deloitte, 2025, "Gen Zs and Millennials at Work.")
> - **Pragmatic career decisions:** While financial stability is a strength, it can also lead Gen Z to avoid risks, missing out on high-reward opportunities that require stepping out of their comfort zones.
> - **Mental health challenges:** Gen Z reports higher rates of anxiety and stress, often linked to economic uncertainties and social media pressures, which can hinder career progression. (See Harmony Healthcare IT, 2025.)

Today's Mid-Career Cohort

Those in the mid-career stage include Gen X (born 1965–1981) and elder Millennials. From a timing perspective, the lines between Millennials and Gen X may overlap; however, Gen X squarely falls into the mid-career stage, while some elder Millennials are mid-career and others are still in their early careers.

Research-Based Generalizations: Gen X

The following are some research-based generalizations about Gen X:

- **Overlooked by leadership:** Generation X often falls into the "forgotten middle child" category, overshadowed by Baby Boomers and Millennials. This lack of recognition can lead to stagnation in leadership pipelines. (See Taylor and Gao, 2014.)
- **Struggles with adaptation to rapid change:** While Gen X is resourceful, the accelerated pace of technological change in recent decades has challenged some members to stay current in their skillsets, particularly with emerging digital tools. (See Pollak, 2020.)
- **Burnout from dual responsibilities:** As many Gen X professionals are balancing demanding careers with caregiving responsibilities for children and aging parents, burnout can become a significant issue. This dual burden can hinder their career advancement and job satisfaction. (See LaMotte, 2014.)
- **Risk aversion:** Having faced multiple economic downturns (e.g., the 1980s recession and the 2008 financial crisis), Gen Xers tend to favor job stability over risk-taking. This cautious approach can limit opportunities for entrepreneurial ventures or bold career moves. (See Antwi and Naanwaab, 2022.)
- **Challenges with networking and social capital:** Compared with Millennials and Gen Z, who are active on digital networking platforms, Gen X may struggle to leverage these tools effectively, potentially missing out on opportunities to expand their networks and advance their careers. (See Free From Burnout, 2022.)
- **Limited mentorship opportunities:** As they occupy mid- to upper-level positions, Gen Xers may find fewer mentors available to guide them, particularly as Baby Boomers retire. This lack of

> mentorship can limit professional growth and innovation. (See Mentoring Resource Center, 2023.)
> - **Resistance to relocation:** Many Gen X professionals prioritize family and community stability, making them less likely to pursue opportunities that require relocation. This resistance can restrict career advancement in industries that call for geographic flexibility. (See Raddon, 2023.)

Conclusion for Millennials, Gen X, and Gen Z

I'm not a big fan of generalizations like the one's I've noted for these generations. They create a stigma that does little but stereotype them. As we move forward, it is essential to recognize and celebrate the contributions of all generations. By understanding the unique contexts in which each generation operates, we can build a more inclusive narrative of success—one that honors the enduring power of grit and social capital while embracing the diversity of paths that lead to achievement. Ultimately, the legacy of these qualities lies not in their static definitions but in their dynamic ability to inspire and propel us toward a brighter future. That is how we all achieve our self-defined *Greatness Objective*.

Redefining Success for the Future

As these younger generations continue to mature, they challenge traditional notions of success and forge new paths that emphasize impact, purpose, and collective advancement. They drive innovations in technology, champion social justice causes, and advocate for environmental sustainability. In doing so, they prove that success is not solely measured by financial wealth or career titles, but also by the ability to contribute meaningfully to the world.

This redefinition of success still aligns with the enduring principles of grit and social capital. While the specific expressions of these qualities may change, their essence remains the same: the determination to persevere and the capacity to build and sustain relationships that amplify one's potential.

5Qs + Social Capital = Greatness

This is the *Greatness Code* formula.

Your Life's Work: The Matterhorn Metaphor

Many will read this book for guidance navigating the stages of their careers. Others will see its applicability in pursuing other *Greatness Objectives* in their lives. Sometimes it's a meandering trail. Other times it's an outright scramble. Let's reflect on what a career journey is all about. How it begins. How it evolves. What it leads to, with its twists and turns, ups and downs, the ultimate peak, and feeling satisfaction during the time period that follows.

My son Chris started his career journey in earnest as employee number 24 at Strategas Research Partners, LLC. Which became a highly respected and influential Wall Street firm. Chris helped build out capital markets, as well as helping to launch their institutional asset manager, and he carved out a niche by working with banks and wealth management institutions. After about a decade cultivating relationships, expanding his industry knowledge, and developing new skills, he was recruited to Citigroup. At Citi, he applied these skills, knowledge, and relationships to the next leg of his career journey. There he forged new relationships, gained broader industry knowledge, and honed his existing skills and developed new skills over several more years.

Then, he took a leap to launch his own firm, Alpine Strategic Partners. This was the culmination of all he experienced up to that point. His first clients were institutions where he had built deep relationships with their leadership in prior years. They had come to trust his advice. He works with firms to help them with their growth strategies, acquisitions/succession planning, business management, and transformation. His relationships across the financial industry enable him to pull in the tools and resources they need to reach their objectives. Chris plans to expand into merchant and investment banking as he continues along the journey. Starting a company is a big risk, but he chose to take that leap.

In 2018, while working at Citi with the long work hours, business travel, and the relentless pressures that come with it, he set a powerful personal stretch goal. He had managed to carve out a week of vacation in Switzerland to meet his objective. He had been building up to it for years—hiking and skiing since he was a kid and climbing since he was a teenager, and then going on treks in the United States and Europe, as an adult. At the time, I was busy and wasn't truly paying attention to his latest trip. One night, while he was in Switzerland, the phone rang. When I answered it, my son said, "I'm going to be out of communication for about 24 hours. Nothing to worry about." I asked, "Where will you be?"

"I'm going to climb the Matterhorn," he said.

To that I responded, "Sure, and I'm gonna' run for president."

I quickly learned he wasn't kidding. Of course, I panicked. I started looking up all of the facts I could on climbing the Matterhorn. As an Army cadet, I attended the Northern Warfare Training Course, so I knew to look up difficulty rating, prominence, height, casualty rate, weather, topography, etc. I then looked at my wife and said, "Who the hell climbs the Matterhorn? What do you think?" Her response: "I think we just need to sit tight until we get photographs from the top of the Matterhorn."

Those photos came, but not until a very long silent period that felt like months. They included photos of my son Chris as he stood at 14,692 feet/4,478 meters atop the Matterhorn, having made it to the peak of the fifth-deadliest mountain in the world, and then back to Wi-Fi in Zermatt, Switzerland.

This wasn't a casual bucket-list adventure. It was the result of years of relentless dedication, a rigorous training regimen, and a mindset shaped by both professional discipline and personal passion. Chris wasn't on a "find-yourself" trek; he was a committed professional with a demanding career, often traveling 20 weeks out of the year. Yet, even on the road, he carved out time to train, frequently before dawn or late at night after a day of meetings. Weekdays meant at least an hour of cardio and an hour on an indoor climbing wall if he was not on the road. Weekends were reserved for 10-plus hours of grueling climbing or cycling. Every step he took, whether up a mountain or into a business meeting, was intentional. For years, he had climbed other smaller mountains from North America to Europe.

Chris had to develop the technical skills required to reach his goal, both personal and professional. New goals require new skills. Climbing on a glacier is different than a cliffside. He studied avalanche safety, crevasse rescue, and new climbing techniques. Some of his studies were from books; other times he learned from climbing guides or partners. The sum of all our experiences teach us what we need to do to succeed. Experience also teaches us not to be distracted by things that are irrelevant or counterproductive to achieving our goal. Over decades of climbing, he acquired the needed knowledge, skills, endurance, and confidence for the next climb. Skills are cumulative, goals evolve, and sometimes we need a partner to reach our objectives.

When climbing, there is no room for error. I asked him once the age-old question, "Why do you climb?" He said, "Work requires me to constantly think about how one thing impacts another. That doesn't stop unless I am fully focused on something else. When I am climbing, I cannot think about where Treasury bond yields are headed. I have to think about where my left foot has to go."

Much like a successful career, to summit the Matterhorn required resilience, courage, stamina, persistence, passion, and meaningful partnership. It's just like the social capital we explore in this book with Ub Iwerks and Walt Disney, Dean Dillon, and a network of amazing performers, Warren Buffett and Charlie Munger, to name just a few examples.

A couple of years before his Matterhorn climb, Chris connected with a professional climbing guide in Europe. Hans was an experienced professional who taught new skills required for high alpine climbing. During our careers, mentors, colleagues, and trusted advisors serve a similar purpose. They don't carry us—they walk with us, challenge us, teach us from their experiences, and keep us sharp. The top of the Matterhorn is only a few feet wide—a combination of snow and rock. The path is like walking on a razor's edge, with a vertical drop of more than 5,000 feet on either side. You have to trust the person you are tethered to and vice versa. Your life quite literally depends on it. That trust comes from experience working together and mutual respect. This social capital takes time to cultivate. Once you have that connection, you don't need to check credentials. You don't need to reaffirm where they are positioned on an organization chart, or vice versa, before working together or extending a helping hand. That's why it is important to build your network before you need it.

Chris often says that a mountain-climbing journey mirrors the arc of a career. Not all professionals start out knowing where they'll end up. We begin with energy and curiosity, taking on roles that stretch us, then another, building capability step by step. Those early climbs Chris and I did when he was a kid—much like entry-level jobs or the grind of mastering new skills—lay the foundation for greater things as we continue our journey. The work may seem thankless or routine at the time, but it builds the stamina, skills, and discipline needed for the ascent ahead.

Of course, the climb is hard. Chris faced unpredictable weather, steep ascents to the 14,692-foot summit, and sheer rock faces. An avalanche took out part of the 8.5-mile trail from the Hornli Hut back to Zermatt the morning they set out for the summit. When they returned to the hut, helicopters, began shuttling climbing teams back to town. It was the only way past the avalanche. A wild ride, yet a silver lininig - it saved them a hike. The choppers hovered off the ground so the climbers could jump out with their gear before the choppers returned for another group. In the same way, careers are marked by setbacks, failed projects, difficult bosses, economic downturns, and many moments of self-doubt. Sometimes what appears to be a setback can actually lead to an unexpected and positive outcome. We may not always see it at the time, which compounds the frustration, but some of our biggest disappointments can lead to the most rewarding outcomes in time. The people who keep climbing are the ones who learn to manage energy, push through discomfort, at times even find new paths, and transform failure into learning.

But persistence alone isn't enough. Passion matters. Chris doesn't climb because he has to; he climbs because he loves the journey and its challenges. Climbing the Matterhorn while working a full-time job on Wall Street was actually about creating balance. It fed something inside him that helped balance the scales. Truly successful people aren't out there to check boxes—they're fueled by purpose, curiosity, and passion. They are doing it to fulfill something in themselves—not to meet external expectations. Chris only told a few people at the climbing gym why he was there with a backpack stuffed with weights as he trained. Even after the fact, only over time did friends and family slowly learned what he had done. He didn't broadcast it. Climbing the Matterhorn is only a little blip in his bio as part of his climbing interests.

You have to want *it*, whatever your *it* may be, because of your own desire—your own reason to put one foot in front of the other and grab something sturdy when you slip. After a lifetime of climbing, Chris knew that reaching the peak is only halfway to a goal. The descent is just as challenging—sometimes more so—and it requires just as much preparation. When it comes to the career journey, Chris has articulated this better than anyone I know. When he works with a client on a mergers-and-acquisition strategy or an executive's business succession plan, he calls this working on their "coming down the mountain strategy." People have to learn to appreciate this phase, ensuring they can reach that career peak, have a lasting result, and live to share their experience with others. The journey to the peak will have a series of smaller victories, such as when Chris and I climbed his first more than 4,000-foot mountain in the Adirondacks as a 12-year-old, or his first peak higher than 4,000 meters in the Alps decades later.

The post-summit phase of a career isn't always about serene retirement—it's a new chapter that requires investment, clarity, and care. You don't simply walk down the Matterhorn. If you don't move with intention in your career transition, you can get hurt—and in the worst cases, it can undermine the peak you achieved. Chris' insight runs counter to a common corporate myth that the summit is the end goal.

I've had more than a few retired executives call me in frustration. They hit their peak, then "retired" to serve on boards, travel the world, work on hobbies, or play more golf. But they're too often unfulfilled. "I'm tired of giving advice," they say. "I want to lead again. I want to build something." The ascent, it turns out, was the fun part. Chris' experience on the Matterhorn is a powerful metaphor for that truth. Your preparation, persistence, and perspective aren't only needed to get to the peak—they are equally needed to come down the mountain with strength, purpose, and the clarity to shape whatever comes next.

A career, like a climb, is about more than reaching the top. It's about how we get there, who we become along the way, and how we carry that growth into what comes next. The journey home is about having the strength and knowledge to share with others, as well as enjoying each step for its own reward. Some people become so fixated on the summit that they forget about the journey and the legacy they can leave behind.

On average about 8–10 climbers die every year attempting to summit the Matterhorn. Approximately 600 have died since the first ascent. Tragically, three climbers died the week Chris summited, and another had to be airlifted to a hospital after falling the day before.

Nothing is certain—your journey may not go as planned. The 5Qs, as part of the Greatness Code formula, Passion, Persistence, Resilience, Courage, and Stamina keep you driving toward your goal every day in the face of setbacks. They help you endure and sometimes enjoy even the most difficult moments along the journey.

The Career Journey: You Build a Foundation

Chris' journey up the mountain mirrors the career path for many. The challenges of the mountain and the workplace may differ in form, but their demands are remarkably similar.

When Chris first started climbing, he did not dream of standing on the Matterhorn's peak. He was simply drawn to the challenge, the adventure, and the discipline required. Similarly, most professionals begin their careers not with a singular, grand vision, but with a desire to explore and grow. Early in our careers, we may not know exactly where we are headed, but we take on challenges, develop new skills, and find areas of passion and competence.

Just as Chris needed to learn basic climbing techniques, aspiring people must develop foundational skills like technical expertise, problem-solving abilities, and interpersonal skills. At this stage, every experience matters. Every small climb, every professional challenge faced and overcome, adds to the base of knowledge and ability that will one day allow for bigger leaps. Many people overlook the importance of these early experiences, dismissing entry-level work or routine tasks as insignificant.

However, much like the physical conditioning required for mountain climbing, these experiences shape the stamina and discipline necessary for long-term success.

Stamina and Resilience: Facing the Climb's Challenges

Mountaineering, like a career, is not without its hardships. Chris encountered steep ascents, unpredictable weather, and moments of exhaustion. He had to develop both mental and physical endurance to push forward when progress seemed impossible. The career journey demands the same. Professionals face setbacks, rejections, failures, difficult bosses, economic downturns, and periods of self-doubt. Resilience is key. Many people give up on their career ambitions when they hit obstacles, assuming they are not cut out for the path they've chosen. But every setback is part of the climb. The true test is whether you have the stamina to endure the tough stretches and keep moving forward after you feel worn down. Much like Chris learned to manage his energy and adapt to challenging conditions, professionals must learn to pace themselves, handle pressure, and turn failures into learning experiences.

Persistence and Progress: The Power of Incremental Growth

Chris took on progressively harder climbs, each one preparing him for the next. He built his endurance, learned from mistakes, and tackled new challenges with each ascent. Similarly, careers are not built overnight. They require continuous learning, skill-building, and stepping into roles that stretch our capabilities.

Persistence is the bridge between ambition and achievement. There will be moments when the climb feels too difficult, when doubts creep in, and when success seems out of reach. But much like a climber taking one step at a time, a professional must focus on steady progress. Promotions, recognition, and mastery don't come immediately, but through sustained effort, professionals move closer to their ultimate goals. Sometimes bad weather rolls in. It's not fair, but you have to deal with it. You need the resilience. You can't complain that others had it easier—unfortunately, unfair breaks will happen. You can quit or you can move ahead. That is in your control, regardless of the weather.

Passion and Courage: Fuel That Sustains the Climb

Chris' passion for the challenge of climbing is what kept him going through difficult moments. If he had seen climbing as a mere obligation rather than a way to personally challenge himself, he would have abandoned it early on. Passion fuels perseverance. Passion sustains ambition. Those who teach themselves to love what they do are far more likely to endure the struggles, setbacks, and sacrifices that come with success. And doing it for yourself, not for others is also key. In a career, passion can manifest as a deep commitment to solving problems, innovating, leading, or making a difference. However, passion is not always immediate. Many people discover it through exploration, much like Chris discovered his love for climbing only after spending time in the mountains. The key is to stay open to experiences, embrace challenges, and recognize when a particular path ignites excitement and motivation.

We all experience fear along the way. Fear of failure is one of the most dominant fears. This can bring on impostor syndrome. Often, we won't take a risk, push back on a plan or a strategy we disagree with, or speak truth to power because we are afraid. Courage is liberating. Fear can be debilitating. Courage is built over time, and it requires a first step. With each risk you take, you learn that you indeed survived. It wasn't as bad as you imagined. Perhaps you had a major failure, but through it, you learned that it wasn't fatal. Time spent pushing through challenges builds the courage muscle. There is an old saying, "We have nothing to fear, but fear itself." This is so very true.

This metaphor touches early, mid, and peak career concepts. It also contemplates what you do after you peak. The journey of coming down the mountain can be as exhilarating as the climb. However, it requires preparation. Even with preparation, it will likely require a period of adjustment. For some, it can be a tough period. We will explore this phase later in the book. Let's now focus more on the early career foundation.

2 | The 5 Qualities (5Qs) in the Face of Early Career Challenges

> Success is the ability to go from failure to failure without losing your enthusiasm.
> —Winston Churchill

The 5Qs must be built over time. In the early phase of your journey, you will meet with painful moments, self-doubt, fear, and many other negative emotions that will challenge you. Some people don't hold up in the face of these challenges, and they derail. Hopefully, with support from a good network around them, they will get back on track. You will not attain a Greatness Objective unscathed.

Persistence: J. K. Rowling—Just Keep Trying

When J. K. Rowling first set out to publish her now-iconic Harry Potter series of books, she was not the successful author we know today. She was an unemployed single mother, typing her manuscripts in small coffee shops while her daughter napped.

Rowling submitted that first manuscript to many publishers, all of which turned her down. Each rejection stung a little more than the last. After 12 turndowns, most people might have called it quits. But Rowling believed in *failing forward*. She saw each setback as a learning opportunity. In her words, "Failure meant a stripping away of the inessential."

Instead of seeing each rejection as a personal failure, she used it as motivation to refine her work, until finally, a small publisher took a chance on her. The rest, as most people know, is literary and cinematic blockbuster history.

The Failure Advantage

For early-career professionals, this *fail forward* approach makes all the difference in the journey toward greatness. The first few years on a job often involve tasks that don't go as planned. Feedback can feel more like criticism and projects often seem to go nowhere.

Reframe the Situation   Learning to reframe each setback as an opportunity rather than a defeat is a critical skill.

With any failed project ask yourself the following questions: What did I learn here? How can I improve next time? When you answer those questions, you will begin to see setbacks, not as obstacles, but as essential parts of the learning and growing process.

The art of reframing setbacks requires a mental shift. Start by viewing each challenge as a valuable piece of feedback rather than a blow to your abilities. Maybe a presentation didn't go well because you needed to prepare more thoroughly. Perhaps a proposal was rejected because it lacked sufficient data. Whatever the case, reframing setbacks as lessons builds mental resilience, a key component of grit.

Dean Graziosi: Having a Greatness Objective—Never Let Go

Many people have heard of Tony Robbins, who is a renowned success. Well until recently, Dean Graziosi was a key leader in driving Robbins' company and is now his business partner.

Graziosi *failed forward* to extraordinary success—not through luck, but through consistent, purpose-driven action, the 5Qs and an amazing ability to build social capital. Today he's a globally recognized entrepreneur, best-selling author, business builder, and personal development leader. But he didn't start there—far from it.

I met Graziosi in 1991. He was in his early twenties, running an auto body shop he'd taken over from his father in Marlboro, New York. From day one, I believed in him. I became his greatest fan and consider him a brother. We've taught each other a lot over the years.

Agility and Ambition   Graziosi's career is a master class in learning agility—the ability to grow from experience, adapt to new circumstances, and turn insight into impact. He didn't wait until he had it all figured out. He started with what he knew and iterated forward.

While running the shop, Graziosi began buying and selling cars as a side hustle, and it turned into a profitable business. Soon, he realized he could empower others to do the same. That insight led to the creation of his first information product, Motor Millions. He packaged what he'd learned, turned it into a repeatable system, and brought it to market.

Overcoming Challenges   Like most breakthrough ideas, Motor Millions didn't take off overnight. Early campaigns fell flat. Money was tight. Criticism was loud. Self-doubt crept in. But Graziosi stayed the course. He doubled down, took on more financial risk, and refined the message and model again and again.

This wasn't blind faith—it was calculated persistence. Graziosi modeled what worked, learned from every failure, and stayed committed to serving the people he knew he could help. Eventually, through late-night infomercials and relentless testing, Motor Millions found its audience. Graziosi had not only created something that helped others, but also proved to himself what was possible.

Real Momentum Motor Millions gave Graziosi the financial foundation to transition into real estate education, where he again focused on teaching everyday people how to achieve financial success with the same strategies he had used. He didn't just pivot—he expanded. His real estate education became the biggest in the nation, doing nine figures annually. Over time, his message evolved from financial tools to full personal development. And his influence kept growing.

Social Capital and Strategic Growth One of Graziosi's greatest strengths is how intentionally he's built social capital—based on authenticity, results, and value. His partnership with Robbins is the best example. Graziosi didn't "get lucky" meeting Tony. He made himself valuable in every room he entered. He led with service first. When they met through mutual contacts, Robbins immediately recognized that Graziosi wasn't just another hustler—he was the real deal that had a depth of caring that aligned with his values.

That meeting started a true friendship that eventually became a partnership. Together, they launched Mastermind.com and co-created the Mastermind Business System—a global movement that now serves millions. Their recent live event had more than 900,000 participants. They've become the gold standard for showing people how to turn life experience into income, impact, and freedom by creating things like courses, workshops, coaching programs and or by becoming a consultant.

Graziosi's role in conceptualizing and promoting this venture showcased his ability to identify emerging trends, leverage partnerships, and create value-driven solutions. The success of the mastermind model further solidified his reputation as a leader in personal development and entrepreneurial education.

Lessons for Future Leaders What I admire most about Graziosi isn't just his stamina or his success—it's his belief that *pain can become purpose* and *purpose can become fuel*. Graziosi has lived what many people are just learning. He says:

- The voice in your head saying you're not ready is just an outdated story.
- Success doesn't require a perfect plan; it requires a *deep enough why*.
- If you model what works and take action, progress will follow.
- Persistence isn't a personality trait—it's a decision you make every single day. It is a muscle you build.

Graziosi once told me:

> The fastest way to success is to model someone else who has already achieved what you want. But that comes with a disclaimer, you have to generate your own hunger to keep persisting. That hunger comes from knowing what's at stake—your family, your purpose, your freedom. That's what turns effort into resilience. That's what creates real growth. Don't wait to feel ready. Model what works. Take messy, uncomfortable action. And never forget why you started.

If you're in the early part of your career, Graziosi's journey holds an important reminder: You don't have to be perfect to start—you just have to start. And when you persist long enough with purpose as your compass, greatness tends to follow.

Become a World Leader: The Sky and Beyond Is the Limit

Greatness Objectives shouldn't face limits. Especially in the early years of a career, don't be afraid to think and dream big. Don't let obstacles stand in your way. Let's learn for Baroness Thatcher.

The Iron Lady—Margaret Thatcher—The Grocer's Daughter

Former UK Prime Minister Margaret Thatcher is a great example of a career and life journey characterized by persistence, resilience, courage, passion, and stamina—the *5Qs*.

Her journey to becoming prime minister was a testament to resilience and political stamina. At every stage, she faced challenges that would have deterred a less determined individual: early election defeats, gender bias, internal party opposition, and relentless public scrutiny. Yet, she never wavered.

Thatcher's persistence in challenging the status quo, her resilience in standing firm amid criticism, and her stamina in navigating the treacherous world of British politics set her apart. She had not only shattered the political glass ceiling, but also laid the groundwork for the sweeping economic and social changes she would later implement as prime minister.

Her story is one of determination against the odds as leader who never backed down and, in doing so, reshaped the course of British history. For those who think that might be far-fetched, consider her nickname and its origins: *Iron Lady*. Early in her role as prime minister, the Soviet press dubbed her that because of her leadership style and uncompromising politics.

Grocery Beginnings My very dear friend Sir Liam Fox served the United Kingdom as a member of Parliament and as a cabinet member under two prime ministers. He is fortunate to have been a close friend and confidant of Baroness Thatcher, from her time as prime minister of the United Kingdom until her death in 2013. I've had the opportunity to hear his fascinating firsthand stories about Baroness Thatcher's determination.

Thatcher's rise from a grocer's daughter in Grantham, England, to becoming the first female prime minister of the United Kingdom in 1979 was marked by relentless perseverance, intellectual rigor, and an unshakable belief in her principles. Her career was not one of easy victories but of overcoming entrenched opposition, proving her worth in a male-dominated political sphere, and standing firm through some of Britain's most turbulent years. From her early days in local politics to her ultimate ascent to 10 Downing Street (the official address of the prime minister), Thatcher demonstrated extraordinary resilience, facing setbacks with determination and using each challenge as a stepping stone to greater success.

Born in 1925, Margaret Thatcher was shaped by a disciplined upbringing. Her father, Alfred Roberts, was a self-made man, a local grocer, alderman, and even mayor, who instilled in her a strong work ethic and a belief in self-reliance. This foundation of diligence and personal responsibility would define her political ideology.

Political Beginnings Thatcher eventually attended Oxford University, where she studied chemistry. Even in her university years, she was drawn to politics, becoming president of the Oxford University Conservative Association. However, as a young woman in post-war Great Britain, she faced significant barriers to entering national politics. Many saw a woman's role in the Conservative Party as limited to local charitable work rather than leadership.

She lost her first two attempts at parliamentary politics but impressed party leaders with her passionate speeches and ability to hold her own in debate. Rather than being discouraged with those losses, she opted to *fail forward* and used these early defeats to refine her political strategy and sharpen her ideological convictions.

Her persistence paid off, though, in 1959 she won the Conservative seat for Finchley, an area in North London, and joined Parliament as one of the few female members. In those early years, as a woman in a male-dominated institution, Thatcher faced skepticism from political opponents and within her own party. But she gained respect with her preparedness and understanding of policy issues. However, it was not until 1970, when Edward Heath became prime minister, that she was given a significant role as secretary of state for education and science. Even then, though, she was often dismissed as the "token woman" in Parliament.

Polarizing Person It was in this role that Thatcher first became a deeply polarizing figure. One of her early and most controversial decisions was to end free milk for schoolchildren over the age of seven as part of budget cuts. The move led to a public backlash, earning her the nickname Thatcher, the Milk Snatcher. The criticism was relentless, but rather than backing down, she stood by her decision.

This episode demonstrated her ability to weather political storms and remain committed to fiscal discipline, a trait that would define her later leadership. Over the years, in and out of 10 Downing Street, Thatcher's resilience and resolve were tested. Often the odds were stacked against her. Repeatedly, many considered her too radical, too abrasive, and/or unelectable or ineffective as a woman.

However, Thatcher had the 5Qs, along with strong social capital and a support group which, when combined with her unwillingness to back down, allowed her to achieve her own *Greatness Objectives*.

Often media and the political establishment doubted her, especially in the early years, whether it was her lack of charisma or broad appeal. Yet, with each challenge she methodically built her case, articulated her visions with ideological clarity, and unwavering belief. This great lady embodied the Greatness Code.

Setbacks in the early stages of a career are not only common but often essential for growth. These challenges provide valuable lessons that shape resilience, adaptability, and perseverance. What truly matters is how you respond—viewing setbacks as opportunities for learning rather than obstacles. Developing the ability to maintain focus, adjust strategies, and stay committed to long-term objectives is key to achieving lasting success. It's the consistency in navigating adversity, along with the ability to rebound with greater determination, that sets apart those who ultimately realize their greatness from those who falter. Embrace the process and stay the course. Stay persistent.

3

Establishing Social Capital Early

> Never lose sight of the fact that the most important yardstick of your success will be how you treat other people.
> —Barbara Bush

The faster you build your network, the faster you get leverage and help others. How do you begin? First, you must want to make connections. You need to be genuine and keep the connections once you make them.

Kevin Systrom: From His Own Connections, an Industry of Connectors Was Born

In 2007, a young computer scientist named Kevin Systrom was working as a product marketer at Google, far from the glamorous world of tech founders and venture capital. At that time, he was simply a talented young man, eager to make his mark. But Systrom had something that would soon set him apart: a network of well-connected mentors and friends who would help him shape an idea that would become Instagram.

Through relationships he had built at Google, Systrom met Mike Krieger, another promising young developer. Their shared background and mutual interests led them to collaborate on Burbn, a location-based app that eventually evolved into Instagram. Krieger's technical expertise complemented Systrom's vision, forming a partnership that was central to Instagram's development. It was a simple idea, but it was Systrom's connections that helped transform that idea into a billion-dollar phenomenon.

Securing Early Investments

Kevin Systrom's ability to build relationships and leverage his network played a crucial role in securing the initial funding for Instagram. While attending a social gathering, he crossed paths with investors from Baseline Ventures and Andreessen Horowitz. Recognizing an opportunity, Systrom seized the moment to showcase the prototype of his photo-sharing app. His pitch sparked interest, leading to a follow-up meeting where he successfully secured $500,000 in seed funding. This early investment provided him with the financial stability to fully commit to developing the app and refining its core features.

Attracting Key Investors and Advisors

Beyond securing initial capital, Systrom's strategic networking attracted influential figures in Silicon Valley who played a vital role in Instagram's early growth. One of these key figures was Steve Anderson, a venture capitalist at Baseline Ventures. Their encounter became a pivotal moment in Instagram's history. After seeing Systrom's early prototype, Anderson not only invested but also provided critical mentorship and guidance during Instagram's formative years.

Another major backer was Jack Dorsey, co-founder of Twitter. Systrom's connection with Dorsey stemmed from his internship at Odeo, a podcasting company. Their existing rapport likely made it easier for Systrom to gain Dorsey's support, resulting in Dorsey's early investment in Instagram. Dorsey's involvement not only infused additional funding into the startup but also helped bolster Instagram's credibility within the broader tech community.

The Power of Social Capital in Instagram's Success

The journey of Kevin Systrom and Mike Krieger in building Instagram highlights the immense value of social capital. While Systrom's technical skills and entrepreneurial mindset were instrumental, his ability to cultivate meaningful relationships ultimately accelerated Instagram's growth. Through strategic networking, he secured crucial investments, gained the mentorship of seasoned investors, and partnered with a like-minded co-founder in Krieger.

Network Resources Equal Social Capital

A study published in *The Economic and Labour Relations Review* in 2024 explores the association between individual social capital and expectations of career advancement. The authors define expectations as "beliefs about a future state of affairs, subjective estimates of the likelihood of future events ranging from merely possible to virtually certain." They argue that these expectations are influenced by individuals' perceptions and can significantly impact career-related behaviors. The study suggests that the ability to mobilize network resources is positively linked with expectations of pay raises and job promotions. The phrase *"mobilize network resources"* refers to the ability of individuals to actively leverage or utilize the connections within their professional or social networks to gain benefits, such as support, information, opportunities, or influence that contribute to their career advancement or personal goals. Who you know may be as important as what you know. This validates my Social Capital premise.

When individuals mobilize network resources, they are effectively drawing on the strengths, knowledge, and support of people within their network. This might include asking for mentorship, seeking introductions to others in the industry, accessing information about job openings, or receiving guidance on how to navigate workplace challenges.

In the context of social capital and career advancement, mobilizing network resources is crucial because it involves converting social relationships into tangible opportunities and advantages. This is distinct from merely having a network; it implies that individuals are actively engaging and utilizing these connections in ways that directly impact their professional growth and outcomes.

The Power of One Connection: The Story of Walt Disney and Ub Iwerks

In the early 1920s, a young, ambitious cartoonist named Walt Disney was struggling to make ends meet in Kansas City. Walt had a knack for drawing, but his business ventures hadn't exactly taken off. He was operating on a shoestring budget, creating short cartoon films in a borrowed studio, when he met a quiet, unassuming animator named Ub Iwerks. Iwerks was a talented artist and skilled animator who was quick to pick up new techniques. But more than that, he was someone Walt could trust—a true collaborator who shared his dream of creating something big.

Iwerks became Disney's first partner and, eventually, the unsung hero behind some of Disney's early successes. Together, they created Oswald the Lucky Rabbit, a character that brought Disney his first real taste of fame. But in a cruel twist, apparently Disney lost the rights to Oswald, and he was left with almost nothing—except his connection with Iwerks.

It was during this challenging time that Disney and Iwerks worked tirelessly to create a new character, one they hoped would bring a bit of magic to audiences. After days of sketching and brainstorming, they landed on a character named Mickey Mouse. While Disney envisioned the character, it was Iwerks who brought him to life, animating Mickey's first cartoons almost single-handedly.

The rest, as they say, is history. Mickey Mouse catapulted Disney into the spotlight, laying the foundation for the empire that would follow. And it was Disney's connection with Iwerks that made it all possible.

For years, Iwerks remained Disney's closest collaborator, helping him innovate and push the boundaries of animation. Their partnership is a testament to the power of social capital—one connection that sparked a legacy.

This story illustrates that success is rarely a solo endeavor. Behind every great achievement, there are often relationships that make the journey possible. For early-career professionals, the lesson is clear: nurture the connections that resonate with you, because you never know where they might lead.

What Systrom, Disney, and many others have shown us is that talent and hard work, while essential, are not enough. The real differentiator often lies in the relationships you cultivate. And these relationships—called social capital—become the bridges to new opportunities, insights, and growth. Social capital is about creating and nurturing genuine connections that not only help you advance but also enrich your career and life.

Expanding Your Network Beyond Your Comfort Zone: Carla Harris Knows

Networking. For many people, the word itself is intimidating, conjuring images of forced conversations at crowded events. But true networking isn't about collecting business cards; it's about building relationships. Early in your career, it's tempting to focus solely on doing a great job and letting your work "speak for itself." But there's a problem with that approach: Work, no matter how good, can only say so much. People need to know who you are and what you're capable of.

People Agility Is Key When It Comes to Social Capital

People agility is the capacity to collaborate effectively with diverse individuals and adapt to different interpersonal dynamics. People-agile individuals excel in teamwork and leadership by understanding and valuing diverse perspectives. Korn Ferry research validates this.

Carla Harris is a prominent figure on Wall Street. She has shared numerous insights with me from her early career that highlight the importance of people agility in relationship building. In her book, *Expect to Win: Proven Strategies for Success from a Wall Street Vet*, she emphasizes the significance of authenticity, mentorship, sponsorship, and the willingness to take risks as key components of career advancement.

Harris recalls that while she initially believed in the meritocratic nature of the workplace—where hard work and intelligence would naturally lead to success—she soon realized that building relationships and having advocates were equally crucial. Being authentic is a key trait in individuals with people agility. In her books, Harris emphasizes the importance of authenticity in building these effective relationships. She writes: "I learned that when you can turn a presentation into a conversation, you have won the battle of converting a client; and second, I learned that the real Carla was my best competitive weapon and my key personal advantage."

A mentor advised her to build a network. Harris, took that advice to heart, making an effort to get to know people across the organization, from junior analysts to senior managers. She joined committees, attended events, and engaged in projects beyond her department. Over time, she built a network that supported her, advocated for her, and finally played a part in propelling her to the role of vice chairman. She underscores the necessity of having a sponsor, someone who speaks on your behalf in decision-making rooms where you're not present. This insight is particularly valuable for professionals navigating complex corporate environments.

In a conversation with Harris, she offered many valuable insights. She stressed that I should also remind people that ambition and work ethic are important fuel in addition to the 5Qs. She shared the following additional insights:

- To expand your own network, start by stepping outside of your usual circles. Attend events, volunteer for projects, and seek out opportunities to meet people from different parts of your organization or industry.
- Instead of thinking of networking as transactional, approach it with curiosity. Ask yourself: Who do I want to learn from others? Who might benefit from knowing me?
- When you see networking as a way to learn and grow, you shift the focus from shortermism to genuine connections.

Her's is great advice born from personal experience. I could not agree more.

Creating Value for Others: The Foundation of Social Capital

There's a saying that goes, "The best way to make a friend is to be a friend." When it comes to social capital, this couldn't be more true. Again, many people approach networking with a "what's in it for me" mindset. But the most successful networkers take a different approach: They focus on creating value for others. They see networking not as a means to an end but as an opportunity to contribute, to listen, and to help.

One remarkable example of this is Adam Grant, an organizational psychologist and bestselling author known for his research on reciprocity. Grant divides people into three categories: *givers, takers,* and *matchers.* Takers are those who focus on what they can gain from each interaction. Matchers operate on a quid-pro-quo basis, willing to help but expecting something in return. Givers, however, operate without expecting an immediate reward. They invest in others, often without any immediate payoff, trusting that these relationships will eventually yield benefits.

In his research, Grant found that givers tend to be the most successful over the long term. They build strong networks because they approach each interaction with a spirit of generosity. This approach to networking might feel counterintuitive, especially early in your career when you feel you have little to offer. But even small acts—like offering to help with a project, sharing useful information, or simply listening with genuine interest—can create lasting value in a relationship.

To start building this kind of value-driven network, ask yourself what you can contribute to each person you meet. Maybe you know someone they should connect with, or you've read an article relevant to their work. Even if you have no immediate way to help, you can still create value by showing appreciation, asking thoughtful questions, and following up. Over time, these small acts of generosity build trust and goodwill, the cornerstones of strong social capital.

A Millennial's Story of the Greatness Code in Action

Sabirul Islam's story goes well beyond simply a tale of a teen turned business success. His journey is a testament to the power of determination, resilience, and connections. He transformed from a teenager with a dream to a global entrepreneur and motivational speaker who has impacted millions globally.

Beginnings

In the bustling streets of London's East End, a young boy, Islam, walked around with dreams far larger than his surroundings. Born to Bangladeshi parents, he was raised in a neighborhood where violence, crime, and limited opportunities could stifle ambition. Yet, from an early age, Islam had an insatiable hunger for success, a passion that refused to be tamed by circumstance.

His journey would be anything but easy, but what set him apart was grit. He had that ability to push forward through rejection, failure, and the weight of expectation. Incidentally, he was also diagnosed with epilepsy at age 11.

As he has written, at the age of 13, while most of his peers were focused on soccer (European football) and video games, Sabirul set his sights on something different—his first job. He was hired by a local newspaper and believed that this was his first step into the world of success. Two weeks later, however, those dreams were crushed when he was fired.

The reason? His work wasn't up to their standard. The sting of rejection was sharp, but Islam didn't let it define him. Instead, he made a decision that would shape his future: He would never let failure be the last word in his story.

Many teenagers would have given up, but Islam saw an opportunity to turn his setback into a strength. If one business didn't think he was good enough, he would build his own. So, at age 14, with a group of friends he launched his first company Veyron Technology—a web design business. He taught himself how to code, worked tirelessly to refine his skills, and started offering services to small businesses in his community. This was his first taste of entrepreneurship, and it taught him an invaluable lesson: Success isn't given—it's earned.

By 17, while others his age were considering university applications, Islam took a different route. He already had enough experience in the business world to know that he wanted more than a traditional path. Instead, he turned his attention to writing.

His first book, *The World at Your Feet*, was a rallying cry for young people to take control of their futures. It wasn't just a book—it was a movement. Nonetheless more than 40 publishers rejected it. So, Islam self-published the book and hit the pavement, promoting it to schools, bookstores, and youth organizations. Within nine months, he sold over 42,000 copies. His message resonated—young people wanted inspiration, and he was ready to give it to them.

Resilience in the Face of Doubt

Despite his early success, not everyone believed in Islam. He faced skepticism from educators, peers, and even within his own community. He was young, ambitious, and unwilling to take no for an answer—a combination that some saw as unrealistic.

But Islam had resilience. For every door that was shut, he knocked on 10 more. For every rejection, he found another way. He understood that success wasn't about avoiding obstacles—it was about overcoming them.

One of the most critical elements in Islam's success, though, was his ability to build and leverage a network. He wasn't content with just being an author. He wanted to create impact at scale. Recognizing the need for financial literacy among young people, he designed the *Teen-Trepreneur* board game, an interactive tool that taught players about entrepreneurship.

But creating a product wasn't enough, either. Islam needed people to believe in it. He reached out to schools, educators, and business leaders, pitching the game tirelessly. His stamina paid off. Soon, the game was adopted by over 550 schools in the United Kingdom and expanded to 14 countries worldwide.

A Network to Amplify Impact

For Islam, business success was just the beginning. He saw a greater mission—to inspire and equip young people across the globe. That vision led to the Inspire1Million campaign, a bold initiative aimed at empowering one million young minds to believe in their own potential.

This wasn't just a motivational tour. Sabirul spoke at more than 800 events across five continents, sharing his journey, struggles, and lessons. He met with young entrepreneurs, business leaders, and change-makers, building an international network of ambitious individuals who, like him, refused to accept mediocrity.

The Legacy of a Fighter

Behind every milestone, success, and headline, Islam achieved was one thing—grit. The journey wasn't a straight road to success; it was filled with failures, rejections, and countless late nights of hard work.

But he never stopped moving forward. He understood that passion alone isn't enough. Stamina—the ability to push through exhaustion, setbacks, and criticism—was crucial. His belief in himself was unshakable, and that belief inspired thousands of others to take charge of their own futures.

Islam's story demonstrates how the 5Qs combined with social capital can be the keys to greatness. It's not about where you start; it's about how hard you're willing to fight for your dreams. Islam fought and won. And in doing so, he showed the world that success is not about luck, privilege, or even talent. It's about the unwavering refusal to give up. And that is the true essence of grit. His awards are many - including Mosaic Entreprenuer of the Year, awarded by the Prince of Wales. The youngest nominee ever at the time.

Emotional Intelligence—The Magic that Makes Relationships

At Korn Ferry, we collaborate with psychologist and bestselling author Daniel Goleman. In my first book, *Smart Is Not Enough* (2007), I wrote about Goleman's research in discussing the notion of a person's emotional quotient (EQ) versus intelligence quotient (IQ), and the value of emotional intelligence (EI). It's impossible to have a conversation with him without walking away having learned something.

Goleman defines EI as a set of skills that enable someone to manage their own emotions and understand the emotions of others. These skills—*self-awareness, self-management, social awareness, and relationship management*—are critical for fostering meaningful relationships. With that in mind, EI provides a powerful framework to understand how to strengthen relationships.

After all, developing social capital isn't just about meeting people and forming connections. It's about building genuine, trust-based relationships that can support long-term success.

Empathy as a Social Connector

A core component of Dan's emotional intelligence model is empathy—the ability to recognize and understand others' feelings. In a professional context, empathy allows individuals to connect with others on a deeper level, making them more approachable and trusted. It's a fundamental leadership skill.

According to Goleman, empathy is the "fundamental people skill" that helps build rapport and creates an environment of psychological safety where individuals feel understood and valued. When professionals show empathy, they not only improve their immediate interactions but also lay the groundwork for stronger, more resilient social capital. Empathy-driven relationships tend to be more authentic and supportive, providing a foundation that can withstand professional challenges.

Building Trust

Another critical element in emotional intelligence is self-awareness, which allows individuals to understand their strengths, weaknesses, and emotional triggers. Self-aware professionals can better manage their responses in challenging situations, promoting consistency and reliability in their behavior.

Goleman notes that self-awareness is closely linked to self-regulation, the ability to control impulsive emotions and reactions. By mastering self-regulation, professionals cultivate a calm, composed presence that others are likely to trust, even during stressful moments. This trust is invaluable when building social capital, as it assures colleagues and clients that they can depend on you, reinforcing the strength of your professional network.

Social Skills Facilitating Positive, Productive Relationships

In addition to empathy and self-regulation, he emphasizes social skills as a cornerstone of emotional intelligence. Effective social skills—such as active listening, clear communication, and conflict resolution—help professionals navigate complex interpersonal dynamics. Goleman argues that social skills are essential for influencing others, managing teams, and building productive, cooperative relationships. Strong social skills amplify social capital by enabling individuals to communicate their needs and intentions effectively while also understanding and responding to others' perspectives.

Emotional Intelligence as a Catalyst for Social Capital

His work reveals that emotional intelligence is an essential catalyst for building and sustaining social capital. By developing empathy, self-awareness, self-regulation, and social skills, early-career professionals can create a network of relationships based on trust, mutual respect, and collaboration. These connections form the backbone of social capital, offering not only career support but also a sense of belonging and shared purpose. Goleman's research underscores that emotional intelligence is not a fixed trait; rather, it's a set of skills that can be developed over time, enhancing one's capacity to connect with others and build a strong, enduring network.

Finding a Mentor

One of the most valuable connections you can make early in your career is with a mentor. That's someone who already has walked the path you're on and can offer guidance, support, and wisdom. A good mentor can help you navigate the challenges of your role, understand the unspoken rules of your organization, and make decisions that align with your long-term goals.

The Case of Warren Buffett

Consider the story of the master investor Warren Buffett, founder of the long successful holding company Berkshire Hathaway Incorporated, and his mentor, Benjamin Graham. In his twenties, Buffett was an eager but inexperienced investor who idolized Graham, a pioneer in the field of value investing. When Buffett had the chance to work for Graham, he absorbed every lesson possible. Buffett was quoted in a CFA Institute article as saying: "And if encouragement or counsel was needed, Ben was there. Walter Lippmann spoke of men who plant trees that other men will sit under. Ben Graham was such a man." Clearly, he was Buffett's mentor.

Graham taught him how to analyze companies, avoid impulsive decisions, and, perhaps most importantly, think independently. Buffett would later describe Graham's mentorship as one of the most influential relationships of his life.

Your Turn Again

While most of us won't have the chance to work with a mentor as famous as Graham, the principles are the same. A good mentor can help you see things that are invisible to others, offer perspective in difficult times, and push you to grow in ways you might not on your own.

To find a mentor, start by identifying people you admire. This might be someone in your organization, industry, or network whose career path aligns with your goals. Once you've identified potential mentors, approach them with genuine curiosity and respect. Instead of asking directly for mentorship, consider inviting them for coffee or a brief conversation about a topic relevant to their expertise. People are often flattered when you show interest in their work, and a casual conversation can be the start of a meaningful relationship.

When you find someone willing to take on a mentorship role, approach the relationship with gratitude and humility. Show up prepared, be open to feedback, and, most importantly, make it clear that you value their time. A good mentor-mentee relationship is built on mutual respect, trust, and a shared commitment to growth.

How can you get a mentor or two? Maybe you can send them this excerpt in an email and ask if they are willing to be for you what Ben Graham was to Warren Buffett. That's an easy way to break the ice if you need to. At minimum, it is authentically flattering!

Strengthening Your Social Capital Over Time

Building social capital isn't a one-time effort; it's a continuous process. Early in your career, every relationship you form becomes part of your professional foundation.

As you progress, these relationships can open doors, offer support, and help you achieve things you couldn't on your own. But like any investment, social capital requires ongoing care and attention.

To maintain and strengthen your network, stay in touch with the people you've met, even if it's just a brief email or message. Celebrate their successes, offer help when you can, and be genuinely interested in their journeys. Over time, these small gestures accumulate, creating a network of people who are not only contacts but allies. I sometimes just send a "no news" text or email. I let them know I'm thinking about them—as indeed I am. Something like *"Hi—I hope you are having a great week. Haven't connected in a while and just wanted to wish you well. Let's chat soon."* It's genuine—I really mean it. I'm not looking for them do anything for me—just want to stay connected. Maybe I can help them—maybe they can help me.

Remember, the goal of social capital isn't simply to build a list of names; it's to create a network of meaningful, reciprocal relationships. By approaching each connection with a spirit of generosity, curiosity, and respect, you create a foundation that will support you throughout your career.

Early Career: A Review

Up to now, in these pages I've offered important suggestions and stories to help most anyone early in their career set themselves up for success and greatness, however you define either. Remember, the choices are personal. Let's briefly review some those elements—the 5Qs:

- **Stamina.** It's crucial to recognize that even though advancement may seem too distant or out of reach, you're in it for the long haul. Like it or not, you are running a marathon, not a sprint.
- **Resilience.** The ability to tolerate setbacks that may come from your mistakes is a must. *Fail forward*, gain experience, and learn.
- **Persistence.** When you encounter roadblocks and resistance, stay in the game. Even though some of that pushback could come from ageism and other dynamics, don't give in to discouragement.
- **Courage.** Stand up to the challenges in spite of any fear of failure or lack of support. It's not as hard as you think. I love the quote often attributed to Mark Twain: "I've experienced some terrible things in my life, some of which actually happened." Basically, your fears are often overblown—just go for it!
- **Passion.** That intensity and determination is what fuels the resilience, persistence, stamina, and courage.
Combine these qualities with a strong network of people to support you, and attaining your Greatness Objective is likely only a matter of time.

4

Early-Stage Exercise

Build Your Foundation and Launch Your Career

> Plans are of little importance, but planning is essential.
> —Winston Churchill

Objective: This exercise is designed to help early-career professionals reflect on their aspirations, explore potential career paths, and lay the groundwork for long-term success.

Help to Get Started: Set aside time to complete a series of guided exercises designed for professionals at the start of their careers. These prompts will help you gain clarity about your direction, surface core motivators, and explore real opportunities that align with your potential.

Drawn from years of coaching and corporate experience, these exercises are designed with time limits to help you think quickly and focus on what matters most. Be honest and reflective—there are no right or wrong answers. The small investment of time will yield valuable insight and momentum for your next step.

Early-Career Playbook: A Five-Step Guide for Early-Career Professionals (Likely Ages 20–39)

Each module provides structured activities to help you explore your goals, build confidence, and take action toward a meaningful, purpose-driven career.

STEP 1: *Discover Your Career Drivers*

Duration: 45 minutes
Purpose: Clarify what energizes and motivates you, so you can align your career path with your values and strengths.

Reflection Questions:

- When do I feel most energized and focused?
- What kinds of people or projects do I naturally gravitate toward?
- What causes or topics do I care deeply about?
- What does success look like for me in the next three years?

Mini Vision Board (Optional):

Create a digital or physical board that illustrates your ideal work life in 5–10 years using images or words. Use tools like Pinterest, Canva, or a simple piece of paper. Name it something meaningful. "My Future"

STEP 2: *Explore and Experiment with Purpose*

Duration: 90 minutes
Purpose: Get curious and begin testing new interests or roles through small, real-world steps.

Career Curiosity List:

List three roles or industries that sound interesting—even if unfamiliar. Alternatively, explore tangential paths within your current industry.

Micro-Experiments—Pick One to Try This Month:

- Reach out to someone on LinkedIn in a role you admire.
- Attend a free webinar or virtual event in that field.
- Take a one-hour online class to test your interest.
- Volunteer or contribute to a project related to that area.

STEP 3: Build Your Skills and Set Goals

Duration: 60 minutes (plus ongoing refinement)
Purpose: Strengthen your résumé and confidence by intentionally growing your capabilities and crafting your personal brand.

Skill Building Plan:
Identify two core skills to develop over the next six months (e.g., public speaking, Excel, UX design, leadership, AI tools, etc.).

Career Story Draft—Answer the Following:
- What experiences am I most proud of?
- What do I want to be known for?
- How do I want others to describe my professional brand?

Use your responses to update your LinkedIn "About" section or practice your elevator pitch.

SMART Goal Exercise

Duration: 30 minutes
Purpose: Learn how to create focused, realistic goals that drive momentum.

SMART Goals Defined:
- **Specific**—Clear and detailed
- **Measurable**—Progress can be tracked
- **Achievable**—Realistic based on current resources
- **Relevant**—Aligned with broader interests
- **Time-bound**—Includes a deadline

Note: The SMART goals framework was introduced by George T. Doran in his 1981 article "There's a S.M.A.R.T. Way to Write Management's Goals and Objectives," published in Management Review *Vol. 70, Issue 11, pp. 35–36.*

Exercise—Create One SMART Goal:
"I will [achieve what], by [deadline], by doing [specific actions]. I'll measure success by [how you'll track it]."

Example:

"I will complete a beginner data analytics course by September 15th by studying for four hours each week. I'll measure success by finishing the final project and adding it to my portfolio."

After writing your SMART goal, share it with a mentor or peer for accountability.

STEP 4: Expand Your Network with Intention

Duration: 1 hour/month

Purpose: Build authentic relationships that provide opportunities and perspective.

Networking Strategy:

- Connect with one new person each month in your field or area of interest.
- Use alumni networks, warm introductions, or LinkedIn.
- Ask thoughtful questions: "What do you love most about your work?"
- Keep a brief log of conversations and key takeaways.

STEP 5: Quarterly Check-In and Recalibrate

Duration: 30 minutes every three months

Purpose: Reflect on your growth, make small adjustments, and stay aligned with your career direction.

Quarterly Check-In Prompts:

- What am I learning about my likes and dislikes at work?
- What progress have I made on my skill or network goals?
- What's one small step I can take next quarter to continue my growth?

Final Output: Career Confidence Dashboard

By completing this playbook, you'll have:

- A clear list of motivators and interests
- A set of micro-experiments completed and insights gained
- A skill-building plan and personal pitch draft

- A starter professional network
- A quarterly habit of reflection and recalibration

I hope you work through each step or selected steps that appeal to you. They are designed to help you reflect on professional aspirations, explore potential career paths, and lay the groundwork for long-term success.

Be honest in your answers. There are no right or wrong things to say. The time commitment will be well worth it.

PART II
Mid-Career: Maximizing Momentum

5 | Leveraging Social Capital for Advancement

Show me a successful individual and I'll show you someone who had real positive influences in his or her life. I don't care what you do for a living—if you do it well I'm sure there was someone cheering you on or showing the way. A mentor.

—Denzel Washington

In the mid-career stage, social capital isn't just about expanding your network; it's about deepening and strategically leveraging connections to open doors, drive growth, and support your career's evolution. Professionals in this phase learn not only to maintain relationships but to amplify their networks by becoming connectors—individuals who are known not just for their own achievements but for actively linking others to opportunities.

In this chapter, we'll explore the steps to transform the relationships you've built into powerful assets for advancement. We'll discuss how to become a connector, build a personal brand, and foster influence—all essential to navigating the unique challenges of the mid-career phase.

Expanding and Deepening Your Network: Quality over Quantity

Early in your career, networking may seem like a numbers game. Conferences, coffee chats, and LinkedIn connections were geared toward meeting as many people as possible. But by mid-career, the focus should shift from quantity to quality. Now, it's time to concentrate on building deeper, more meaningful relationships with the people who matter most—your social capital.

Take the approach of Reid Hoffman, co-founder of LinkedIn. "Opportunities do not float like clouds in the sky. They are attached to people. If you are looking for an opportunity, you're really looking for a person," – wise words often attributed to him. Reid also has emphasized the importance of what he refers to as a *small world network*.

Instead of building a vast number of superficial contacts, invest in a select group of people you respect, trust, and value. Reid's network wasn't just about getting ahead; it was a mutually supportive ecosystem where people helped one another grow. When he needed advice, introductions, or partnerships, his network was there, ready to provide support.

To build your own small world network, focus on key relationships that will add value to that person's career as well as your own. Start by identifying individuals in your professional life who have been helpful, inspirational, or influential, and then make a conscious effort to reconnect with them. Set up periodic check-ins, lunches, or calls. Deepen these connections by offering your support, sharing insights, or collaborating on small projects. By consistently nurturing these bonds, you create a strong core network that can provide you with invaluable support in your mid-career journey.

Becoming a Connector: Creating Value by Connecting Others

In the mid-career phase, one of the most valuable roles you can play within your network is that of a *connector*. Connectors are individuals who don't just benefit from relationships; they actively create value by linking people who can benefit from each other. By introducing individuals in your network who share interests, goals, or complementary skills, you establish yourself as someone who fosters opportunities and strengthens community.

Adam Rifkin has been recognized as a leading super-connector in various publications. As far back as 2011, *Fortune* magazine described him as the best networker in Silicon Valley. Additionally, the book *Superconnector* by Scott Gerber and Ryan Paugh highlights Rifkin's exceptional ability to forge meaningful professional relationships.

Adam dedicated time each week to making introductions between people in his network, often with no immediate benefit to himself. He firmly believed that helping others succeed was valuable in its own right. Over time, these introductions came back to benefit him, as people sought him out for advice, opportunities, and partnerships. Rifkin's philosophy was simple: By being generous with his connections, he amplified his social capital and influence, becoming a well-regarded hub of knowledge and resources.

I developed another approach to network building, codified with the help of a great thinker, George Bradt, a friend of mine and the author of *The New Leaders 100-Day Action Plan: How to Take Charge, Build Your Team, and Get Immediate Results* (Wiley, 2008). During a 2009 brainstorming session with George for a paper I was working on about relationship selling, I coined the acronym ICARD, which stands for *identify, connect, approach, reapproach, and deliver*. (It was after the debut of the iPhone, and I thought ICARD sounded catchy.) Table 5.1 gives you an overview of the process.

Table 5.1 **The ICARD Process Summarized**

Step	Description
Identify	Determine who you want to add to your network.
Connect	Find a way to get introduced to that person.
Approach	Approach that person through the connection.
Reapproach	Follow up in some way to open a meaningful connection.
Deliver	After the reapproach deliver on whatever you and that other person sought to do.

I have used this methodology hundreds of times since 2009. Business relationships are fine, but they are formal. Personal relationships are powerful. Whenever possible, when I meet a business contact I really like, I truly work on creating a friendship. This is easily done by opening up to them in a personal way. Share details about your family. Engage in conversations about challenges you're facing—don't let it be *all* business. You will quickly determine who is open to this connection and who isn't. If they don't reciprocate, they are probably not a great match for you—just not the right chemistry. If that's the case, you simply have a business connection. That's the next best thing—but having a business friend is better.

To use ICARD to develop new business, each year I would look at various lists of successful people relevant to my work. This could include lists of the "Forty Under Forty" in fintech, or Fortune's "Most Powerful" in finance, among other lists. This is the *identify* step. Then I would make an effort to find people in my network who could introduce me to people on my list and help me *connect*. I prefer this be an invitation to something social—*not* a business meeting. These introductions would happen, leading to the *approach*. Sometimes it was an initial meeting for drinks, or to attend a sporting event. Then, after that interaction, I would follow up in some way to solidify the connection, or sometimes, they would follow up with me. This is the *reapproach*. I just walked you through the first four steps of ICARD.

After the reapproach, it works well if they ask you for something. In my case, it may be career advice or help they need with their business. Whatever it was, it gave me the opportunity to *deliver*. I provided my assistance as a friendly accommodation, and that deepened the relationship. Eventually, this put me in a position to ask them if there were ways my company could meet and discuss a business relationship. You also gain a real friend. That is where the magic is.

To summarize, you sincerely connect with them on a personal level. Likely, you can be helpful in some way. Then, after you have that friendly rapport, you can easily segue into the business connection. Clearly, this doesn't happen overnight lets put this into a list with one of those bold vertical bars you have used to highlight content in chapter one. it will break up the page nicely. However, it does happen, and in my case, leads to decades-long relationships that have been personally and professionally gratifying. At this point, the line between being friends and clients is totally blurred. That's the best relationship. It is one built on mutual trust and shared vulnerability.

The ICARD model is equally useful in building a support network of mentors and others who can help you achieve your *Greatness Objective*. Remember, this requires you to be genuinely committed to the relationship. This is a two-way street where you benefit from each other.

It's Your Turn

To work with connectors and become a connector, start by identifying potential matches within your network. Who might benefit from knowing each other? Perhaps you have a colleague who's looking for a graphic designer, and a friend in another department who specializes in digital design. Maybe someone in your network is launching a project that could benefit from the insights of a former mentor. Facilitating these introductions establishes you as a valuable resource and cultivates a reputation as someone who creates opportunities for others.

As you make connections, focus on quality over quantity. Introduce people thoughtfully, with a genuine sense of how they might benefit from knowing each other. Briefly explain the context and your reason for introducing them, so they understand the value you see in the connection. The ripple effect of these introductions can be far-reaching, enhancing not only your social capital but the overall strength of your network.

Building a Personal Brand: Define Your Value

In the mid-career phase, a strong personal brand is crucial for differentiating yourself and standing out. A brand can communicate your skills, expertise, and values to your network and beyond. A strong personal brand isn't just about self-promotion; it's about establishing a reputation for the unique qualities and skills you bring to the table. With me, for example, I published a book, *Smart is Not Enough*, in 2007. I wasn't that concerned about the number of copies sold, though it did well. What mattered most was that a major publisher branded me a credible expert on career success. And that attracted clients.

Consider Oprah Winfrey, one of the world's most recognized and respected personal brands. When she launched her career, Winfrey didn't simply aim to be a talk show host. She was clear about her mission: to use her platform to inspire and uplift others. This commitment became her brand's foundation, allowing her to build an empire based on authenticity, compassion, and influence. Her brand was clear, consistent, and inspiring, helping her attract audiences, collaborators, and eventually, the resources to create her broadcast network, OWN.

The Details

For mid-career professionals, building a personal brand takes intentionality. Start by reflecting on your values and strengths. What do you want to be known for? What makes you stand out? Once you've defined your brand, consistently communicate it through your work, your interactions, and your presence online. This might mean sharing industry insights on LinkedIn, taking speaking opportunities, writing a book, or even developing a personal website or blog to showcase your expertise.

Building a personal brand takes time, but with clarity and persistence, you can shape a reputation that speaks to your strengths and differentiates you in your field.

Strengthening Your Influence: The Power of Strategic Alliances

In the mid-career phase, influence becomes a vital factor in advancing and achieving larger career goals. One of the most effective ways to build influence is through strategic alliances—relationships with others who can champion your ideas, collaborate on projects, and open doors to new opportunities.

Consider the strategic alliance between Warren Buffett and Charlie Munger. In the 1960s, Buffett met Munger, a lawyer and investor who shared his passion for disciplined, value-based investing. Over time, their partnership would transform Buffett's approach to investing, shaping him into one of the world's most successful investors. Munger's perspective and insight were invaluable to Buffett, as they challenged and expanded each other's thinking. The strength of their alliance allowed them to build Berkshire Hathaway into a powerhouse, benefiting from each other's skills, ideas, and support. Munger served as vice chairman of Berkshire Hathaway from 1973 until his death in 2023.

For professionals, forming strategic alliances means finding individuals whose strengths complement your own. This might be a colleague with expertise in a different area, a mentor who understands the industry landscape, or a friend with connections that could support your goals. Approach these alliances with a collaborative mindset, offering help and support where you can. As these relationships deepen, they become mutually beneficial sources of advocacy, partnership, and influence.

In my case, I had the opportunity to meet with the board of the Federal Reserve Bank of Philadelphia as they were seeking to recruit a new president. A role like this literally impacts the world. In addition to being the president of this critically important institution, the person in this role also is a rotating member of the 12-person Federal Open Markets Committee (FOMC). The FOMC, among other things, sets the Federal Funds Target Rate, which directly affects market interest rates for the United States, and influences rates across world markets. To compete for this project, as is almost always the case in my industry, I needed a key partner. In this case, it was my friend Nels Olson. Nels co-leads our Board and CEO Services Practice at Korn Ferry and had been involved in several high-profile CEO succession projects for influential organizations and companies within financial services with ties to agencies in Washington, DC. This type of credibility, coupled with my expertise in financial markets and CEO search, became the winning combination needed to be selected for this project. My alliance with Nel began years earlier. That is key. You must build your network before you need it.

To strengthen alliances, communicate openly and consistently. Share your goals, listen to their aspirations, and look for opportunities to work together. Strategic alliances are built on trust, mutual respect, and a shared commitment to growth. These relationships often become pillars of support and influence, helping you navigate complex challenges and open doors that might otherwise be closed.

Persistence Along the Entire Career Journey—But Especially in Mid-Career

Chris and John: A 40-Year Climb of Persistence and Innovation at Every Career Stage Forty years ago, Chris and John Pappas took over their dad's small business. But from their father; they also learned about work ethic and a set of values. From there, after years of hard work, they earned a front-row seat in New York City's vibrant restaurant scene. From New York, they eventually spanned the country and beyond. They brought with them a vision far beyond their father's reach: to reinvent the role of a food distributor. Instead of merely delivering ingredients, the brothers set out to become strategic partners to chefs and restaurateurs—curators of fine foods, marketers of culinary excellence, and trusted advisors in the fiercely competitive hospitality industry.

That vision would go on to transform a modest family business into Chefs' Warehouse—now the largest specialty food distributor in the United States, and a global player with an expanding footprint. The company's mission: to empower culinary professionals by delivering the world's finest ingredients with service, insight, and a passion for food.

A Corporate Culture of Grit and Growth

Running a business like this one is not for the faint of heart. Over four decades, there probably wasn't a week where Chris and John didn't have to summon extraordinary reserves of resilience, persistence, courage, stamina, and passion (5Qs) just to survive—let alone grow. Whether navigating volatile food markets, managing the logistical complexities of perishable goods, or adjusting to the ever-evolving demands of elite chefs, the brothers operated in a pressure cooker of constant change. Chris Pappas put it plainly: "Integrity and perseverance are essential qualities when joining the Chefs' Warehouse team. It's a 24/7 industry, you must have the stamina to fight every day." Their growth story is extraordinary. From 2010 to 2025 alone, the company added over $3.5 billion in revenue. But the true hallmark of their leadership is not just how they scaled the business—it's how they endured the storms that would have sunk most others.

The Leverage of Social Capital Fueled Their Success

Social capital was one of the most critical ingredients in their success. You cannot grow a business this quickly at this scale organically. It requires multiple acquisitions each year. The businesses they bought were typically smaller distributors of specialty foods or specialty product companies that were often run by families. It took years of building relationships with many of these owners for them to get the opportunity to ultimately buy these businesses. This wasn't just about whether they would pay more than anyone else, it was about the owners of these businesses, trusting Chris and John with their family's legacies.

The same is true for their relationships with the chefs. I don't think there is a renowned chef in America that doesn't see them as friends and trusted business partners. The social capital they established with these chefs and other customers was a critical success element. Theirs is a relationship business. Customers can choose from a universe of providers—but making customers into friends and allies helped Chris and John reach their Greatness Objective.

Then Came COVID-19

When the COVID-19 pandemic hit in 2020, the Chefs' Warehouse was among the hardest-hit businesses in America. They were considered an "epicenter business." I know the intimate details because I served on their board of directors at the time. Virtually all of their core clients—restaurants, cruise lines, hotels, casinos, and entertainment venues—shut down overnight. Their addressable market plummeted to zero. Imagine running a multi-billion-dollar enterprise and waking up to a day when your customers stop ordering—indefinitely. In that moment, the 5Qs they had developed—courage, passion, persistence, resilience, and stamina—were tested like never before. They pivoted quickly, redirecting operations to serve small grocery chains where demand was soaring. They preserved cash, protected jobs where possible, and worked closely with their board to make decisions guided by principle, not panic. Their foundational belief in grit and adaptability helped them survive the most devastating crisis of their professional lives.

An Enduring Legacy

In 2025, the Chefs' Warehouse celebrated its 40th anniversary with a special edition of its quarterly magazine. The pages didn't just reflect on revenue milestones or operational highlights—they told a richer story, one written by the world's top chefs. Full-page testimonials from culinary luminaries across the globe shared personal stories of trust, collaboration, and admiration for what Chris and John had built. Many called the Chefs' Warehouse indispensable to their success. As one chef described in the commemorative edition: "They are always moving forward. This mindset and perseverance are the cornerstone of CW's success and continue to inspire me every day."

Under Chris' leadership and John's operational stewardship, the Chefs' Warehouse has become more than a distributor—it's a cornerstone of the modern culinary world. It has redefined what it means to be a partner in hospitality and proved that heart, hustle, and vision can feed a movement.

In every great dish, there is a story behind the ingredients. In the case of the Chefs' Warehouse, the story behind the story is one of grit, humanity, and a relentless commitment to excellence. And after 40 years, they may just be getting started.

Chris and John have proven that you can set big goals and, by realizing it's a journey and not a sprint, you can ultimately reach your Greatness Objective. Consider their story: In their twenties, they started a business. From that point through to their sixties, they took serious hits, certainly must have gotten tired at times, and indeed faced many business threats that required courage and persistence.

The 5Qs are behind every success story. Trust this insight and invest in yourself—develop these qualities. Again, social capital becomes the multiplier in the success formula. These personal connections are strategic alliances when they are fully formed.

Navigating the difficult middle years of a career is often where long-term success is forged. The 5Q muscles built in the early-career phase give you what you need to succeed. In this phase, professionals face complex projects, shifting expectations, and increasing responsibility. Those who endure and adapt find that the lessons learned become the foundation for later achievements. Stamina allows you to persist through heavy workloads and setbacks without losing momentum. Courage empowers you to take calculated risks, champion new ideas, and lead even when outcomes are uncertain. By combining social capital with persistence and bravery, mid-career challenges become stepping stones instead of roadblocks, ultimately propelling you toward your career peak. Chris and John Pappas illustrate the art of the possible. Learn from their story. Mid career is your launch pad to the peak.

Wall Street Is Not an Easy Place to Play

If you own a stock, have an IRA, or a 401(k), you can probably thank Richard J. Daly for keeping you informed. Daly founded and built Broadridge Finanacial Corp, through relentless resilience, deep passion for service, and unwavering perseverance.

Daly Was Not a Pampered 1980s Wall Street Executive

He began as a hard-working, scrappy accountant and eventually became a rising star in the brokerage industry. Throughout the book, we have talked about the 5Qs: persistence, resilience, courage, passion, and stamina. I haven't talked enough about innovation, which is table stakes when it comes to truly standing out. However, innovators are often ahead of their time, meeting lots of resistance and skepticism. Only a few persist and emerge over years of challenges.

Daly's journey began at the beginning of his mid-career phase in the late 1980s, when—as an experienced Arthur Andersen CPA who had risen to COO at Independent Election Corp and held senior roles at major brokerages—he envisioned transforming proxy-mailing services by offering white-labeled investor communications under brokerages' names. He secured funding from investor Arthur Long, only for Long's untimely passing to imperil the venture. Taking a big risk, because he wasn't wealthy, Daly personally funded the software development after Long's demise. The Arthur Long connection was a critical social capital connection that Daly the confidence to move ahead.

Charles Weber is a person whom Daly credits for his contribution to the launch of Broadridge. An extra bedroom in Daly's home served as its initial headquarters. Upon bringing Weber on as a 9 percent partner in charge of systems, Daly jokes that *World Headquarters* moved to Weber's basement. Daly was the visionary. Weber brought a strong tech background. Technology expertise enabled rapid system development by using Realia-COBOL software to write mainframe code on a PC—cutting edge in 1988. After failing to raise venture capital, Daly sold his startup to ADP in 1989, yet remained resolute, immediately signing 31 clients in his first two years at the firm. Over the next 10 years, annual revenue went from $0 to over $1B.

At ADP, Daly poured more than $100 million into building state-of-the-art printing and distribution facilities, processing millions of envelopes daily—all in service of scaling his vision for efficient investor communication services. His grit showed most clearly during the 2007 spin-off. At a Pierre Hotel roadshow, facing skeptical investors, Daly pledged to "disrupt ourselves before we let anyone else disrupt us"—articulating a bold commitment that corporate governance would evolve radically under his leadership.

When the 2008 global financial crisis hit, rather than cutting staff, Daly doubled down on investment: transitioning 80 percent of paper communications to digital, expanding global markets, embracing digital and cloud technology early, and growing the back-office business (GTO) from annual decline to consistent growth under then-COO Tim Gokey. Today, According to Daly, GTO processes over $8 trillion per day in security transactions worldwide. As he said: "We're going to provide people access to information and execute transactions efficiently and easily on whichever digital device they prefer."

That combination of long-term thinking and operational discipline underpinned Broadridge's transformation into a fintech leader—and secured its status as an S&P 500 company with multi-billion-dollar revenue. But it took courage in the face of uncertainty to take the risks this move required courage—the muscle Daly built over his early career.

Throughout, Daly's passion for rewarding shareholders by empowering his staff to exceed customer expectations played a big part in solving the "investor engagement crisis in America"—fueled by product innovations like digital platforms for ProxyVote™, Realia-COBOL™, and Wealth In Focus™, which transformed investor participation.

Every company needs commercial DNA. Rich knew Chris Perry from his industry network. Rich leveraged that key social capital connection and personally recruited Chris to super-charge the next phase of commercial growth. Chris eventually became President of Broadridge. Daly's career exemplifies how social capital combined with grit leads to success. From founding against odds, investing through crisis, to reshaping a legacy back-office business into a modern, digital fintech champion, the challenges were clearly there. According to Daly, the majority of financial communications that investors receive today are powered by Broadridge.

I have seen many smart people get to leadership roles and fail. They can't share the spotlight; they can't showcase others' contributions; it has to be ALL about them. Eventually, this lack of self-awareness becomes a derailer. No matter how much grit or determination you possess, surrounding yourself with the right colleagues can elevate your potential and multiply your impact. Talent and perseverance are essential, but it's the support, insight, and shared ambition of a strong team that often determines whether you succeed or fall short. The right people challenge you, sharpen your thinking, and fill in the gaps where your strengths end. In many cases, the difference between breakthrough success and frustrating failure isn't effort alone—it's who's standing beside you. I can't finish this story without mentioning my dear friend Bob Schifellite who passed away too soon. Rich mentored Bob, and Bob ran and grew Broadridge's biggest business unit for many years. Greatness is rarely a solo journey; it's built through collaboration, trust, and shared commitment. Rich Daly proved that.

6

Cultivate Lasting Grit

> Success always demands a greater effort.
> —Winston S. Churchill

The 5Qs that you have built and strengthened are now key pillars in your formula for success. Building them is one thing, but using them in a lasting way will get you through your mid-career to your eventual peak.

Charity Adams: A Mid-Career Standout in the Middle of a War

Charity Adams' story is a profound mid-career example of the 5Qs. She used them to help overcome racial and gender barriers while making history in the U.S. Army. As the first Black female officer in the Women's Army Auxiliary Corps (WAAC) and later the commanding officer of the 6888th Central Postal Directory Battalion, she displayed extraordinary tenacity in the face of systemic discrimination, hostile environments, and overwhelming logistical challenges. Her leadership and determination helped revolutionize military logistics and paved the way for greater inclusion of Black women in the armed forces. Adams' incredible story exemplifies all that's explored in this book. Now her story and that of her fellow soldiers has been retold in the 2024 Netflix movie *The Six Triple Eight*.

Born on December 5, 1918, in Kittrell, North Carolina, Adams was raised in a family that placed a strong emphasis on education and resilience. Her father, a Baptist minister, and her mother, a schoolteacher, instilled in her a deep sense of discipline, perseverance, and faith.

From an early age, Adams faced racial segregation and limited opportunities due to Jim Crow laws, which enforced segregation and discrimination. However, she excelled academically, graduating as valedictorian from Booker T. Washington High School. She then attended Wilberforce University, a historically Black college, where she majored in mathematics, Latin, and physics, a rigorous combination that demanded focus and discipline. Despite the societal pressures that discouraged Black women from pursuing higher education, she persisted, graduating in 1938.

Adams initially began her career as a teacher, but she aspired to serve on a broader scale. When World War II created new opportunities for women to contribute, she saw her chance, despite knowing that military service would present unique challenges for a Black woman.

In her memoir, *One Woman's Army: A Black Officer Remembers the WAC* (1989), she writes that her military journey began through her connection to the dean of women at Wilberforce University. This proved to be a critical social capital connection.

When Adams enlisted as a soldier in 1942, the WAAC (later relabeled the WAC) had only been established that year, and its leadership was reluctant to recruit Black women. She knew that by joining, she was stepping into an institution that may not openly welcome her. A major test of her grit came during officer training at Fort Des Moines, Iowa. The military was still segregated, and Black women officers faced immense scrutiny. Some white officers refused to acknowledge them as equals.

Despite these challenges, Adams excelled, becoming the first Black woman commissioned as an officer in the WAAC. She was then assigned as a training supervisor at the WAAC training center, where she quickly developed a reputation for discipline, intelligence, and strong leadership. But she was also keenly aware of the racial tensions in the military.

By 1945, the Army recognized her leadership abilities and assigned her to command the 6888th Central Postal Directory Battalion, the first and only all-Black, all-female unit to serve overseas during World War II. Their mission? Clear a massive backlog of undelivered mail that had piled up—more than 17 million pieces—addressed to U.S. troops in Europe.

The assignment was daunting: The mail system was in complete disarray, with undelivered letters and packages stacked to the ceilings of warehouses. Conditions in war-torn Europe were brutal. The women had to work in freezing, rat-infested warehouses with little rest. They faced skepticism and hostility from both white male officers and local communities that were unaccustomed to seeing Black women in leadership roles. They were expected to fail. Few, if anyone, believed they could clear the backlog in the six months they were given.

But Adams refused to be defeated. She instilled discipline, efficiency, and morale among her soldiers, motivating them to push through fatigue and discrimination. The women of the Six Triple Eight worked in three shifts, 24/7, with no days off, and they completed the backlog in three months, half the expected time.

As the story is told, at one point, a white general attempted to intimidate Adams by suggesting that he would send a white male officer to oversee her command. Her response? "Over my dead body, sir."

She stood firm, refusing to relinquish her authority. The general backed down. Her determination set a precedent. Black women could and would lead in the U.S. Army. In her memoir, she quotes that general as later saying, "It's been a long time since anyone challenged me, black or white, but you took me on. You outsmarted me, and I am proud that I know you. I would not have told you this if I thought I would ever see you again."

Despite proving herself under extraordinary circumstances, Adams knew that her career in the Army would likely be limited due to institutional racism. After the war, she chose to leave the military. She went on to earn a master's degree in psychology from Ohio State University and spent the rest of her career advocating for education and civil rights.

Adams' grit not only broke barriers for Black women in the military but also helped pave the way for desegregation in the armed forces. Her leadership directly contributed to the growing push for Executive Order 9981, which President Harry Truman signed in 1948, officially desegregating the U.S. military.

Today, the 6888th Battalion has been honored with congressional recognition, and Adams' contributions are increasingly being acknowledged. Her story is not just about military successes, but also perseverance, unshakable resolve, and refusing to accept limits imposed by others. She shattered racial and gender barriers, all while leading with excellence. Her journey proves that grit fuels people to rise to challenges, stand up to injustice, and create a path for those who follow.

Brad Arington: A Millennial Building Greatness One Dog at a Time

Success doesn't follow a single path. While some professionals rise through corporate ladders, or the military, or non-profits, others begin in the trades or hands-on roles that call for manual labor and also demand grit, problem-solving, and adaptability. Many inspiring careers start in so-called "manual labor" fields—electricians, mechanics, railroad workers, or construction workers—who later pivot to launch businesses, lead teams, or consult in their industries. Their early experience grounds them in real-world challenges and often gives them a practical edge in entrepreneurship. These transitions remind us that career success isn't defined by where you start, but by how you learn, adapt, and leverage your experience to create new opportunities. Brad Arington's story is a fine example of this.

I've had the privilege of knowing Brad Arington personally. Watching his journey up close for over a decade has helped validate the Greatness Code principles. Arington's rise from humble beginnings to national recognition is impressive, but what struck me most is how he embraces a deeper definition of success—not just as a business leader, but as a husband, father, and mentor.

Arington's story begins in the humid stretches of South Georgia. Raised by a single mom in a modest trailer, he learned early that hard work wasn't optional. Though their resources were limited, the household was rich in values like stamina, resilience, and the belief that effort yields results.

As a teenager, Arington had an special connection with animals. In a region where horses were part of life, he stood out for his ability to read their subtle cues and train them through patience and persistence. But it was the region's demand for bird dogs that sparked a business idea: If he could train horses, why not retrievers?

In 2003, Arington scraped together scraps of fencing and built his first dog kennel in the backyard. It was rudimentary, but it was a start. And it all came together around Bo, an unremarkable dog in pedigree, but the perfect first student. Arington trained Bo through countless hours of repetition and trust-building. The dog's transformation became Brad's first proof that passion and persistence could create excellence.

Arington wasn't drawn to school, but he was a standout baseball player—disciplined, competitive, and driven. When it came time for college, he made a choice. He turned down the opportunity to play baseball and took a railroad job instead. It provided steady income while he nurtured his dream quietly on the side.

In his early twenties, Arington married his high-school sweetheart, Ellen. She became his life and business partner. From the beginning, Ellen supported, managed, and believed in his dream. Together they built the foundation of what would become a nationally recognized dog training brand, Mossy Pond—all while raising four children.

A vital influence in Arington's life was his father-in-law, who served as a mentor and role model. Working closely with him, Arington learned the kinds of lessons you don't get in classrooms—how to show up, persist, and finish what you start.

Evenings and weekends were dedicated to dog training. Word spread. One dog became four, then more. Arington's reputation grew faster than his backyard could hold. Friends and strangers alike sought him out, drawn by his results and unique approach.

Arington's method was different. He didn't train dogs through fear or dominance—he built partnerships. He respected each dog's instincts and energy, taught them through trust, and shaped them into confident performers. This became the Mossy Pond method: firm but fair, patient but purposeful.

By his mid-twenties, Brad realized he was no longer running a hobby—he was building a life. He founded *Mossy Pond Retrievers* and left the railroad behind to go all-in on entrepreneurship.

The early years were filled with risk and uncertainty. The Aringtons invested everything—time, money, and energy—into growing the business. Arington expanded, borrowed, bought land, and built infrastructure. Each fence and kennel stood as a symbol of his persistence. There were plenty of fears—failure, foreclosure, losing clients—but he pushed forward.

Today, barely 40 years old, Arington leads an operation that spans hundreds of acres of South Georgia countryside. Mossy Pond Retrievers has grown into a world-class facility, training hundreds of dogs with on-site lodging, dining, and hunting grounds. What began as a backyard hustle now employs a professional team that upholds the same values and expertise.

Accolades followed. Mossy Pond dogs have taken top honors at the ESPN Super Retriever Series. Arington didn't chase recognition—it found him. Brands like Orvis, Yeti, Benelli, Eukanuba, and others now proudly associate with his level of excellence. His personal brand—rooted in grit and trust—opened doors to high-profile customers and, eventually, the financial capital needed for expansion.

Arington's journey reflects all five of the Greatness Code's core attributes: passion, resilience, stamina, persistence, and courage. But it also highlights the sixth, essential factor—social capital. His relationships built on mutual respect and shared ambition made the impossible possible.

In 2011, Arington made a key connection—my wife Kathy, owner of Saint Hubert's Lodge and Sporting Clays Club in Marlboro, New York. Arington needed a way to train dogs year-round, but Georgia's summer heat was a limiting factor. Kathy offered an opportunity to expand Mossy Pond to the Northeast. Their partnership, grounded in shared values and trust, resulted in Mossy Pond Retrievers New York—a strategic extension that dramatically expanded Arington's reach.

But perhaps Kathy's most profound impact wasn't business-related. She challenged Arington to reflect on what greatness truly meant. While he aspired to someday enter the Field Trial Hall of Fame, Kathy posed a deeper question: "Which Hall of Fame matters more—the Field Trial Hall of Fame, or the father and husband Hall of Fame?" It was a simple yet transformative moment. Arington has often said it was the most important advice he ever received. It reframed his pursuit of greatness—not just as achievements, but as character and legacy at home.

Sometimes social capital helps us grow professionally; other times, it helps us grow personally. It can be the mentor who advocates for your promotion or the partner who reminds you what matters most.

Mossy Pond also needed capital. As the business outgrew bank resources, Arington turned to investors. His reputation and brand had earned him friendships with country music stars and influential figures in the gun dog world. Some early investor attempts fell short, but eventually, he found the right partner—someone who believed in his vision and values. That partnership allowed Mossy Pond to hit its tipping point.

The 5Qs alone wouldn't have gotten him there. It was social capital—relationships and reputation—that led to investment capital and brought the formula together. Arington's story is proof that greatness isn't handed down or bought. It's built—patiently, persistently, piece by piece—by those brave enough to believe that humble beginnings are just the first chapter in a much bigger story.

The formula remains clear: 5Qs + Social Capital = Greatness. The Aringtons live it every day. For mid-career professionals, the takeaway is this: Grit keeps you in the game, but your connections are what help you level up.

Table 6.1 offers advice to mid-career professionals on how to maintain grit, have vision, and use social capital in this phase of their careers.

Table 6.1 The Keys to Mid-Career Growth as You Head Toward the Peak

Key Point	Advice	Actionable Steps
Clear Goals	Revisit and refine your career objectives to ensure alignment with long-term aspirations.	Reflect on your career trajectory. Identify areas for growth. Set specific, measurable, and time-bound goals.
Resilience	Cultivate mental toughness by learning from setbacks and staying adaptable to change.	Practice mindfulness and stress management. Reframe challenges as opportunities. Seek constructive feedback.

(continued)

Table 6.1 (Continued)

Key Point	Advice	Actionable Steps
Continual Learning	Invest in personal and professional development to remain relevant and engaged.	Take courses or certifications. Read industry-relevant books and articles. Attend conferences or webinars.
Continual Building and Leveraging of Relationships	Strengthen your professional network and leverage it for support, guidance, and opportunities.	Join industry groups. Schedule regular check-ins with mentors. Actively participate in professional communities. Use the ICARD method (Chapter 5).
Purpose and Passion	Reconnect with the passion that drove you to your career. Explore new dimensions of your role.	Reflect on what excites you about your work. Volunteer for projects that align with your interests. Pursue hobbies that complement your career.
Time Management	Prioritize effectively to balance work, life, and growth opportunities.	Utilize productivity tools. Delegate tasks where possible. Schedule downtime to recharge.
Health and Well-being	Maintain physical and mental health to sustain energy and focus.	Incorporate regular exercise into your routine. Adopt a healthy diet. Practice gratitude and work-life balance.

Key Point	Advice	Actionable Steps
Celebrate Milestones	Acknowledge your achievements to stay motivated and build confidence.	Maintain a journal of accomplishments. Share successes with peers or mentors. Reward yourself for milestones.
Stay Persistent	Stay committed to your goals even when progress is slow or obstacles arise.	Break large goals into smaller tasks. Review and adjust plans regularly. Surround yourself with supportive individuals.

The 5Qs—persistence, stamina, courage, resilience, and passion—aren't traits to summon only in moments of crisis or ambition. They are daily disciplines, essential to sustaining progress toward your goals. True success isn't built on occasional bursts of effort but on consistent application of these qualities, even when no one is watching. Passion fuels your drive, persistence keeps you moving, stamina endures the long haul, resilience absorbs the setbacks, and courage helps you take the next bold step. Together, they form a mindset—one that must be practiced every day. Greatness isn't a moment; it's a commitment you renew and cultivate constantly.

7

Mid-Career Exercise

Reassess, Stay the Course, or Realign Your Path

> The greatest danger in times of turbulence is not the turbulence—it is to act with yesterday's logic.
> —Peter F. Drucker

Objective: This exercise helps mid-career professionals take stock of where they are, assess how their strengths fit with evolving opportunities, and chart a deliberate course toward their career-related Greatness Objective(s).

Help to Get Started: Set aside uninterrupted time to work through the prompts and frameworks that follow. These exercises encourage honest reflection on what energizes you and where you create the most value. Each section is timed to help you focus without overthinking. There are no right or wrong answers—only insights to guide your journey.

Mid-Career Playbook: A Five-Step Career Strategy Sprint Designed for Mid-Career Professionals

Each module incorporates evidence-based frameworks, real-world application, and structured outputs to produce tangible results.

STEP 1: *Strategic Self-Inquiry — Your Career Thesis*

Duration: 60 minutes (including journaling and a peer debrief)
Purpose: Move beyond surface-level reflection to articulate a "Career Thesis," a hypothesis that connects your identity to value creation in the world.

Prompted Deep Dive

Answer in a dedicated journal or digital document:

- What energizes me intellectually, emotionally, and physically at work?
- What patterns emerge when I've been at my best?
- What core problem or opportunity do I feel most compelled to solve in my industry or community?
- When others seek me out, what is it they count on me for?

Career Thesis Format

Draft a single sentence that starts with:

- "I create value by . . ." This is your "edge"
- "My work matters because . . ."
- "Over the next ten years, I will contribute to the world by . . ."

Peer Debrief (Optional but Powerful)

Collaborate with a some colleagues for a 20-minute session:

- Share the points in your thesis and have them challenge it with "Why?" "So what?" and "For whom?"
- Refine your statements based on the conversation.

STEP 2: *Market Scan & Personal Moat Analysis*

Duration: 2 hours
Purpose: Assess where the world of work is going—and how your edge fits in.

A. Industry & Trends Briefing

- Research two intersecting trends relevant to your interests (e.g., AI in finance, sustainability in consumer goods).
- Use analyst reports, insights from consulting firms, podcasts, or sector newsletters.
- Create a short one-slide summary: Trend → Implication → Opportunity.

B. Personal Moat Map

Using a 2 × 2 matrix, identify:

- What you're world-class at
- What you're passionate about
- What the market values
- Where you have credibility or unique access

The intersection is your personal moat—your competitive advantage.

Here's a simple example of how you might build a Personal Moat Map using a 2 × 2 matrix. In this hypothetical case, imagine a mid-career professional with a finance background who is passionate about sustainability:

World-Class Skills	What You're Passionate About
Financial modeling and analysis	Sustainable investing and ESG research
Market Values	**Unique Access/Credibility**
Expertise in green finance, risk management and regulatory compliance	Deep network within environmental NGOs and government agencies, plus a track record of advising on public-private partnerships

How to interpret the matrix:

- In the *World-Class* quadrant, you list the skills and capabilities where you consistently outperform peers. In this example, that's advanced financial modelling.
- Under *Passion*, note the topics or fields that energize you—in this case, sustainable investing.
- In the *Market Values* section, describe trends or skills that employers or clients are willing to pay for, such as green finance and regulatory expertise.
- Finally, in *Unique Access*, capture any relationships or credentials you have that are hard to replicate—for example, a strong network among environmental NGOs and regulators.

Drawing from all four quadrants of the matrix in this example, this individual's personal moat can be expressed as follows: they leverage world-class financial-modelling expertise and a passion for sustainable investing to create value in the rapidly growing field of green finance. By combining deep knowledge of risk management and regulatory compliance with unique relationships across NGOs and government agencies, they are exceptionally positioned to guide public-private partnerships and ESG initiatives that others cannot easily replicate.

The intersection of these elements helps you identify your "personal moat": the combination of excellence, passion, market demand, and privileged access that sets you apart and guides your future opportunities.

STEP 3: Opportunity Design Lab

Duration: 90 minutes

Purpose: Prototype potential futures by testing ideas through real-life action and dialogue. Strongly consider your current employer as your growth platform. Only leave if a new opportunity is hugely compelling.

Option Prototyping Framework Pick three career directions or role evolutions that intrigue you. You will need to be familiar with the Future-Back framework. A future-back scenario is a strategic planning method that starts by imagining a specific, desirable future outcome and then works backward to identify the steps needed to get there. For each of the three scenarios, write a mini "future-back" scenario. For example: "It's 2029. I'm working as a [role] in [company/sector], and I spend most of my time doing [X]. I'm valued for [Y], and I'm developing [Z]."

Tactical Testing: Rapid Prototyping Your Preferred Scenario After selecting the most promising scenario, test it quickly and purposefully through small, low-risk experiments. The goal isn't to commit to a massive career change overnight, but to gather real-world feedback before making a bigger leap.

Choose **one** of the following actions and commit to it over the next 30 days:

1. **Conduct Three Informational Interviews**
   Identify three individuals currently working in roles or industries related to your top scenario. Reach out for 20- to 30-minute conversations to explore:
   - What a typical day looks like.
   - The skills and credentials that matter most.
   - Any surprises and challenges they didn't anticipate.
   - Their advice for someone pivoting into this space.

   Purpose: To gain unfiltered, insider insight and build connections.

2. **Join a Community of Practice**
   Find a professional association, networking group, or online community where people in your target role or industry exchange ideas. Look for:
   - Industry-specific LinkedIn groups.
   - Slack or Discord communities.
   - Local meetups or national organizations.

   Purpose: To immerse yourself in the language, challenges, and culture of this potential new path. Passive exposure builds tacit knowledge and relationships.

STEP 4: Build a One-Year Roadmap for Strategic Momentum

Duration: 75 minutes (plus biweekly 15-minute check-ins)
Purpose: Create not just goals, but positioning milestones.

Goal Categories

1. **Reputation Goals:** Speak on a panel, publish a piece, mentor.
2. **Capability Goals:** Gain a credential, master a tool.
3. **Access Goals:** Build strategic connections.

SMART Goal Refinement

Duration: 30 minutes
Purpose: Transform intentions into structured, high-impact outcomes using the SMART framework—specific, measurable, achievable, relevant, and time-bound.

Exercise: Set Two SMART Goals

1. Capability Goal:
   "I will [develop X skill] by [date], by doing [method of learning]. I will measure success by [project, certification, or demonstration of skill]."

   Example: "I will improve my executive presentation skills by October 1st by joining a speaking cohort and giving two presentations at work. Success = high ratings from peers."

2. Reputation or Access Goal:
   "I will [publish, speak, or connect with] by [date], by [action step]. I'll measure success by [engagement or visibility outcome]."

   Example: "I will publish a LinkedIn article on AI in fintech by August 15th. I'll measure success by receiving at least 500 views and 10 comments."

STEP 5: *Executive Calibration + Reframe Sessions*

Duration: 30 minutes quarterly
Purpose: Stay aligned, adaptive, and calibrated to your evolving purpose.

Quarterly Leadership Journal

Answer:

- What bet did I place this quarter?
- What surprised me?
- What do I now know that changes my thesis or roadmap?

360° Recalibration (Optional)

Ask two or three trusted peers:

- "Where do you see me adding the most value?"
- "What do you think my next big play should be?"
- "What do I need to get better at?"
- "How are my people-skills?"

By completing this exercise, you will lay a foundation for pursuing and tracking progress toward your objectives.

PART III

Career Peak: Sustain Success and Leave a Legacy

8 | Navigating Leadership with Grit and Social Capital

I fight on, I fight to win.

—Margaret Thatcher

In the later stages of a career, it's easy to feel like you've "arrived." You've established yourself, earned recognition, and perhaps even reached the financial security of your dreams. But the people who maintain grit in their peak years know that true fulfillment comes from continually setting new goals.

The Long Game

At the height of her career, Maya Angelou was celebrated as a poet, author, and activist, with a string of bestselling books, awards, and honors to her name. By any measure, she had reached the pinnacle of success. Yet even at the peak of her career, she didn't change her approach to her work. She continued to wake up before dawn, write diligently each day, and maintain a fierce dedication to her craft. In her book, *Wouldn't Take Nothing for My Journey Now* (1993), she writes, "Success is loving yourself, loving what you do, and loving how you do it." To Angelou, grit wasn't just about reaching a goal; it was about staying engaged, curious, and committed to excellence, even when she had little left to prove.

Reaching the peak of one's career often brings a unique set of challenges. While the early and mid-career years require grit to overcome obstacles and establish a foundation, the later years call for grit to sustain motivation, avoid complacency, and stay passionate about one's work. Questions many professionals often ask themselves, include, "How do I stay excited about my work?" and "How do I continue to grow when I've already achieved so much?"

Richard Branson, co-founder of the Virgin Group, helped build a business empire spanning music, airlines, telecommunications, and even space travel. With each success, Branson could have comfortably retired. Instead, he chose to keep expanding, exploring industries that intrigued him, and challenging himself in new ways.

For professionals in the peak years of their careers, the willingness to reinvent oneself can be the difference between stagnation and continued growth. New goals don't have to be as drastic as founding a new company or venturing into space. They can be as simple as mastering a new skill, taking on a mentorship role, or exploring ways to give back through philanthropy. Setting goals that are challenging yet aligned with your values keeps you engaged and ensures that your work remains fulfilling.

To cultivate grit through reinvention, first identify areas that excite you. What have you always wanted to try but haven't yet explored? Whether it's launching a side project, writing a book, or learning a new technology, setting fresh goals ensures that your career remains a journey of growth rather than a destination.

Role of Lifelong Learning in Sustaining Grit

In a world that's constantly evolving, lifelong learning has become essential to maintaining relevance and resilience. Those who sustain grit throughout their careers understand that knowledge and skills are never static; there's always something new to learn.

Lifelong learning is about more than professional development; it's about keeping your mind engaged and fostering curiosity. For those at the peak of their careers, learning doesn't have to be confined to work-related subjects. Many successful people find renewed grit by exploring new fields, hobbies, or intellectual pursuits. Learning keeps someone mentally agile, adaptable, and open to fresh perspectives—all traits that become invaluable in a rapidly changing world.

To integrate lifelong learning into your routine, dedicate time each week to read, take courses, or attend workshops. Look for topics outside of your immediate field to spark curiosity and broaden your worldview. This commitment to learning not only fuels personal growth, but also inspires others, and creates a culture of curiosity and resilience in those around you. By the way, if you are a business professional, now may be the time to go earn a PhD. If you are a tradesperson, perhaps it's time to get a degree in engineering, or a certification in a new or related specialty area such as HVAC, electrical design, architecture, construction management, or labor relations.

Staying Curious: The Power of a Beginner's Mindset

One of the keys to lasting grit is to maintain a sense of curiosity, even in areas where you're highly accomplished. Curiosity—often described as a *beginner's mindset*—allows you to approach problems with openness, humility, and a willingness to learn. "I am always doing that which I cannot do, in order that I may learn how to do it." That's a beginner's mindset! That quote, often attributed to artist Pablo Picasso, encapsulates the essence of growth—pushing beyond comfort zones to develop new skills and capabilities. It aligns perfectly with the principles of resilience, perseverance, courage, and stamina that mid-career professionals need to embrace.

When someone constantly engages in challenges that stretch their abilities, they continue to learn and reinforce the mindset that failure is a part of the process. It's also a powerful approach to building social capital. When a person tackles new things, they also position themselves to meet and collaborate with others who can support, mentor, and open doors. Even after achieving fame as one of the most celebrated painters of his generation, Picasso continued experimenting, challenging conventions, and pushing his creative limits.

Curiosity prevents complacency, keeps you energized, and allows you to see familiar situations through a fresh lens. For peak-career professionals, a beginner's mindset fosters resilience by helping you embrace uncertainty and approach challenges with excitement rather than dread.

To cultivate a beginner's mindset, practice asking questions and exploring topics that fall outside your comfort zone. Attend talks, read books on unrelated subjects, or engage in discussions with people from different backgrounds. When you allow yourself to be curious, you keep your work dynamic and engaging, and sustain the grit needed to navigate new challenges.

Giving Back: The Role of Purpose in Maintaining Passion and Stamina

Many professionals reach a point in their careers where they start to look beyond personal success and consider the impact they want to have on others. Purpose—knowing that your work contributes to something greater than yourself—can be a powerful source of motivation. It's no coincidence that many peak-career professionals find renewed energy and grit when they mentor others, support social causes, or share their knowledge.

In 2024, I spoke with Bill Gates in New York. I was super happy for a chance to chat one on one. (Shamelessly, I took a selfie with him, too. He's one of the many CEOs I admire but have not worked with.) Later that evening, he was speaking at an event where a participant asked him what he would have done differently in his time at Microsoft. Gates shared some very specific thoughts about major things he could have done differently. His answer proved that even when you reach his level, you know there could have been more.

After stepping away from the CEO role at Microsoft, he dedicated his time and resources to the Gates Foundation. He clearly found renewed purpose in addressing global health and poverty issues. Philanthropy provided a new chapter, one where his grit and determination could be channeled toward a larger mission.

Even if someone can donate only time instead of money, they can still work for important causes. For peak-career professionals, giving back takes many forms. It might involve mentoring junior colleagues, volunteering, or working on projects with a social impact. Finding purpose in this work can reignite a passion and provide a fresh perspective on a career. It's a reminder that grit isn't just about personal achievement, but also about making a difference in the world.

To incorporate purpose into your career, think about the legacy you want to leave behind. What causes resonate with you? Who could benefit from your guidance and expertise? By aligning your career with your values and purpose, you create a source of grit that sustains you even during the toughest challenges.

Balancing Ambition with Fulfillment: Find Contentment Without Complacency

In the peak years of a career, there's often a delicate balance between ambition and fulfillment. Professionals who sustain grit know how to balance the drive for continued success with a sense of contentment and gratitude for what they've already achieved. This balance helps prevent burnout and allows them to enjoy the journey rather than constantly seeking the next milestone.

Again, consider Oprah Winfrey, who reached monumental success as a media mogul, actress, and philanthropist. While she continued to take on new projects and explore different interests, she also made time to practice gratitude and find joy in her accomplishments. For Oprah, balance was about recognizing her achievements and knowing when to pause, reflect, and recharge. Her story serves as a reminder that ambition and fulfillment can coexist and fuel each other, rather than compete.

To find this balance in your own career, cultivate practices that help you appreciate your accomplishments while keeping your eyes on the future. Reflection exercises, journaling, and mindfulness practices can help you stay grounded and relieve the pressure to constantly prove yourself. When you find contentment in your current success, you build the emotional resilience to pursue new challenges without losing sight of what you've already achieved.

Building Your Legacy: Defining What Lasting Impact Means to You

In the later stages of a career, the concept of legacy often becomes more significant. Legacy isn't just about professional achievements, but also the impact a person leaves behind for others, the lessons they impart, and the values they instill. Professionals who continue to cultivate the 5Qs understand that their legacy is a reflection of their character, resilience, and commitment to continued growth.

U.S. Supreme Court Justice Ruth Bader Ginsburg in her later years continued to fight tirelessly for justice. Her legacy wasn't defined by a single case or ruling, but by her unwavering dedication to equality, her resilience through personal and professional challenges, and the influence she had on generations of lawyers and activists. For her, the legacy was about creating a lasting impact and ensuring that her work would continue to inspire change long after she was gone.

Lynn Martin: Achieving a Peak and Building a Legacy

I have known and worked with Lynn Martin for many years. She recently roasted me at my birthday party in front of about 60 people. Her ascent to the 68th president of the New York Stock Exchange (NYSE) is a testament to her unwavering grit and the strategic cultivation of a significant professional network. Her journey from a computer science enthusiast to a leading figure in global finance underscores the power of perseverance and the importance of building meaningful relationships and also making a career pivot.

Raised in Smithtown, New York, Martin developed an early interest in technology, often experimenting with her family's Commodore 64 computer. Encouraged by her father, an electrical engineer, she pursued a bachelor's degree in computer science at Manhattan College, graduating Phi Beta Kappa in 1998. Her academic journey didn't stop there; while working at IBM, she earned a master's degree in statistics from Columbia University, balancing professional responsibilities with rigorous academic demands.

Martin began her career at IBM, where she worked as a computer programmer, developing complex code and managing projects within the financial services sector. During this period, she recognized the significance of networking, building relationships with colleagues and industry professionals that would later prove invaluable. One of her project managers at IBM would leave Post-it notes on her computer with helpful reminders such as "You can never over communicate." The small acts of recognition stuck with Lynn as a powerful way to support a team and encourage clear and consistent communication.

In 2001, due to her deep interest in the mathematical models that drive financial markets, Martin joined the London International Financial Futures and Options Exchange (LIFFE). This move marked her entry into the financial markets, where she took on roles that demanded both technical acumen and strategic insight. Her tenure at LIFFE was characterized by her ability to navigate complex financial instruments, build strong customer relationships and her commitment to continuous learning, often seeking mentorship from seasoned professionals to deepen her industry knowledge. She also made an important Social Capital connection when Tom Callahan, CEO of NYSE Liffe U.S. recognized her potential. As markets began to digitize, Martin's computer science background became invaluable. Not only could she understand deeply complex technology, but she also had the gravitas to convey these topics to a room of executives.

This role also marked the beginning of her journey with NYSE Group, as LIFFE and its parent company, Euronext, became part of the NYSE in 2007. Just a few years later, the NYSE was acquired by Intercontinental Exchange (ICE), a technology and data powerhouse that provides services across major asset classes, helping customers access workflow tools that increase transparency and efficiency. The leaders at ICE recognized Martin's talents, appointing her as Chief Operating Officer of ICE Clear U.S., where she oversaw clearing operations.

In 2015, and as a result of the continued digitization of markets, ICE started a new division, ICE Data Services, and named Martin president. ICE quickly decided to acquire Interactive Data Corp (IDC) as a cornerstone of the business. She stewarded the division through a competitive time for the indices landscape, where new competitors with innovative products were entering the market. To combat these evolving threats and seize on additional opportunities associated with passive investing, ICE acquired Bank of America's suite of indices in 2017, allowing the data services business to grow and differentiate its offerings. Through this process,

Lynn learned the importance of knowing your strengths as a company and continuously identifying new opportunities that compliment these strengths. It took courage to take the big step in acquiring IDC.

Lynn's successful career was not without obstacles. Navigating the male-dominated financial industry required resilience. She was often one of the few women in executive meetings, a scenario that demanded confidence and assertiveness. Lynn addressed these challenges by focusing on her financial and technological expertise and her ability to consistently deliver results, thereby earning the respect of her peers. Her grit was evident in her willingness to take on complex projects, and under her leadership, Lynn doubled the ICE Data Services business' growth rate, generating revenue of $1.9 billion in 2021.

Later that year, Martin received a call from ICE Founder and CEO, Jeff Sprecher, asking her to run the New York Stock Exchange. By accepting the position, Martin became the third woman to hold this prestigious position in the exchange's more than 230-year history.

Her appointment was a culmination of years of hard work, strategic networking and a deep understanding of both technology and finance. As president, she oversees the world's largest stock exchange, a role that involves stewarding the U.S. capital markets and engaging with global business leaders and policymakers. Lynn took the helm at an uncertain and volatile time for markets. After a blockbuster year for IPOs in 2021, rising interest rates, geopolitical tensions, and recession fears caused IPOs to halt, leaving many to question when new public issuance would return. The fiercely competitive industry required her to demonstrate the 5Qs—courage, resilience, persistence, stamina, and passion.

Never afraid of a challenge, Lynn led the exchange through this period and remained committed to bringing new companies to market. Two years later, under her leadership, the NYSE led the reopening of the IPO market with significant deals, including Viking Cruises, StandardAero, and Reddit.

In keeping with peak career precepts, Martin is also dedicated to identifying and mentoring the next generation of leaders at ICE and the NYSE. Throughout her career, Martin had mentors who have challenged her with new stretch roles that she may not have felt fully qualified or ready for. She describes these experiences as transformational for her career, allowing her to reach new heights. As president of the NYSE, she has adopted this practice as her own, cultivating the next generation of talent and giving them new opportunities and roles they may not have expected. Lynn believes that her biggest obligation as a leader is to set the organization up for continued success by developing young talent and building a strong bench.

Martin's story is a powerful example of how with grit and a well-cultivated network, the pinnacle of success is possible. Her journey underscores the importance of perseverance, continuous learning, and the power of strong relationships. As she leads the NYSE into the future, Lynn's career serves as an inspiration for leaders across industries.

To define your legacy, think about the values you want to pass on and the influence you hope to have. Your legacy might be your contributions to your field, your role in supporting future leaders, or the positive changes you've made in your industry. By focusing on your legacy, you give purpose to your efforts and create a source of grit that sustains you, even in the later stages of your career.

Sustaining Grit Beyond Your Career

The 5Qs are more than a collection of qualities; they are a mindset that influences every aspect of a person's life. When someone cultivates lasting grit in their career, they're also preparing for the challenges, changes, and opportunities that lie beyond work. Whether you transition into full retirement, take on advisory roles, or explore new interests, the grit you've developed will serve you well in navigating life's later stages.

When grit is a lifelong practice, the peak years of a career aren't an endpoint; they're a chapter filled with growth, contribution, and impact. Each challenge, goal, and accomplishment becomes part of the larger journey that continues to evolve, inspire, and create lasting value. Sustaining grit extends beyond success. It comes with embracing the journey, staying curious, and leaving a legacy of resilience, passion, and purpose.

Leadership is often described as a journey rather than a destination. It's a role that requires constant adaptation, an unwavering commitment to growth, and, perhaps most importantly, the grit to persevere through challenges. A leader's influence is not simply a function of their title; it's built through resilience and the relationships they foster. For leaders, grit is a foundational quality that allows them to guide others through difficult times.

Social capital, meanwhile, is the network of trust and influence that empowers leaders to inspire, collaborate, and make lasting change.

Grit in a Peak-Stage Leader: Persevering through Adversity and Executing Strategy

The 5Qs manifest differently in a seasoned leader compared with early- and mid-career professionals. That's because the challenges each career stage faces are different. Yet, all require grit to persevere. I always tell dissatisfied junior professionals, that the pressure will be with them throughout their careers. When I tell them that CEOs may be the loneliest and some of the most frustrated people I know, they're shocked. They think it gets easier as you move up. After all, CEOs are in complete charge; but that's a myth.

One of the great things about my job is that I am someone CEOs can talk to safely. I'm not on their board of directors. I'm not their employee. I'm just a connected third party with the benefit of seeing many companies and many CEOs and learning from them. Acting as a sounding board, truth teller, and a frank, constructive critic, I can pass on what I have learned to these leaders.

Most people have trepidations when they talk to a CEO. I get to be unvarnished and tell them what I observe and think. My next promotion or bonus does not hinge on them, so it's safe for me to be open. If I am accurate in my observations, they benefit from hearing from me and my colleagues. We tell them things that others won't.

For example, when I told a recently appointed CEO that the group he referred to as his *executive team* actually was not yet a team, he was taken aback. I shared with him that his direct reports were not harmonized, but siloed. While they referred to themselves a team, they didn't actually work together with the enterprise in mind.

I then stressed that, in this scenario, the only people who woke up in the morning thinking about growth across the enterprise were his chief financial officer and him. Everyone else was looking only at their specific units. None would sacrifice from their budgets to underwrite more valuable enterprise growth that could come from another division. None would export some of their best talent to another unit for the good of the enterprise. Was that a team working with interdependence to drive the enterprise forward? I think not.

I learned a month later that he had asked at least two executive team members how they felt about the cohesiveness of the *team*. It was now on his mind. Not long after that, he began investing in team effectiveness, and more importantly, paying closer attention to individual behavior for the good of the enterprise.

Leaders require the strength to address uncomfortable topics. After all, few people thrive on change or accountability. But this is what leadership grit looks like. Leadership is often romanticized as a position of control and direction, when in reality, it frequently involves learning to navigate uncertainty and manage crises. The most resilient leaders are those who apply the 5Qs not only to advance their own goals, but to keep their teams motivated and focused on a shared mission.

James Gorman and Morgan Stanley – Persistence, Passion, Stamina, and Resilience

While I never worked directly with James Gorman, I admired his work and we exchanged an occasional email. Morgan Stanley was a big player in the markets I covered. James Gorman's story exemplifies grit in several key ways beyond simply strategic foresight. His journey at Morgan Stanley involved a persistent, resilient approach in the face of deep internal and external challenges, and it was his tenacity and willingness to stay the course through adversity that illustrated true grit.

When James took over as CEO in 2010, Morgan Stanley was grappling with the aftermath of the 2008 financial crisis. The firm faced significant challenges, including declining revenues, a tarnished reputation, and intense regulatory scrutiny. Morgan Stanley's stock price had plummeted from over $80 per share in 2007 to under $15 in early 2009, reflecting the market's skepticism about the firm's ability to recover. James inherited an organization struggling to find its footing in a rapidly changing financial landscape, and his leadership would be tested at every turn.

James approached the situation with a tenacious resolve, implementing a bold, long-term strategy focused on stabilizing and transforming Morgan Stanley's business model. Recognizing the need to reduce reliance on volatile trading revenue, he shifted the firm's focus towards wealth and asset management, a sector with more predictable income streams. This transformation required James to make difficult decisions, such as implementing cost-cutting measures, restructuring the firm's divisions, and making substantial investments in technology to improve client experience.

This strategic shift began to pay off. Between 2008 and 2020, Morgan Stanley's wealth management division grew significantly, driven by James's acquisition of Smith Barney from Citigroup. By completing this transaction that valued the business at $13.5 billion, Morgan Stanley became one of the largest wealth management firms in the world, overseeing $4 trillion in client assets by 2020. Wealth management revenues rose steadily, from $7 billion in 2008 to $19 billion in 2020, contributing 40% of the firm's overall revenue. This transformation into a wealth management powerhouse helped make Morgan Stanley's earnings less volatile and more resilient during economic downturns.

James's journey wasn't without setbacks. The shift toward wealth management was initially met with skepticism, and restructuring efforts faced early challenges that tested his patience and resolve. In the first few years, the firm's stock price remained under $30, as investors were unsure about the long-term impact of his strategy. Yet, James's commitment to his vision and his belief in the need to adapt to a new market reality never wavered. His grit was evident in his focus on the long game, persisting through criticism and doubt.

Under James's leadership, Morgan Stanley ultimately emerged stronger. By 2020, the company's market cap had soared to over $120 billion, a testament to the success of James's strategic transformation. Morgan Stanley's stock price, which had hovered around $20 per share at the time of James's appointment, rose to $100 per share by the end of 2021, signaling renewed investor confidence. Additionally, the firm's return on equity—a key measure of profitability—improved from under 10% in 2010 to nearly 15% by 2020.

James's grit was not just about overcoming the immediate crisis but about redefining the company's future and instilling a resilient, forward-thinking culture. Leaders like James show that grit in leadership is not only about facing adversity head-on but about transforming challenges into lasting opportunities for growth and adaptation. His story is a testament to the power of resilience, strategic foresight, and an unwavering commitment to a transformative vision. Some would say this example just shows how smart James was — and not about grit. However, consider these points and you will see the focus and tenacity that was required, beyond being smart.

- **Commitment to a Vision Amid Skepticism:** When James made the decision to pivot Morgan Stanley's focus toward wealth and asset management, many were skeptical. Shifting a firm known for its trading prowess into a more stable, lower-margin business was seen as a gamble. Yet James maintained his conviction in the strategy despite pushback from some stakeholders, demonstrating his ability to stay committed to a long-term vision, even when it wasn't popular. This steadfast focus, especially when success was not immediately visible, reflects grit.
- **Facing Financial and Operational Setbacks with Resolve:** The restructuring of Morgan Stanley's divisions and the full integration of Smith Barney took longer and proved more complex than initially expected. Operational setbacks and the need to overhaul systems for a new business model required a steady hand and a deep well of resilience. James faced these obstacles without wavering on his approach, addressing each challenge with measured steps rather than giving in to pressure for quick fixes.
- **Navigating a Difficult Regulatory Landscape:** The post-2008 era introduced stricter financial regulations, which put additional strain on Morgan Stanley's resources. James's leadership through compliance overhauls, regulatory requirements, and adapting to increased scrutiny required endurance and patience. His ability to navigate these regulatory demands without derailing his broader strategic vision was a testament to his resilience.
- **Driving Cultural Change Through Persistent Leadership:** James's transformation involved changing not just Morgan Stanley's business focus but also its internal culture. Moving a firm's identity from a high-stakes trading mentality to a client-centered wealth management mindset involved reshaping its culture and required his ability to influence employees' perspectives. James had to build trust with his teams and inspire buy-in for a vision that was vastly different from the firm's previous path. Persistently championing this shift in culture showed his

commitment to a new identity for Morgan Stanley, which demanded patience and resilience over time.

- **Rebounding from Criticism and Staying the Course:** In the early stages of his tenure, James's strategy didn't yield instant success, and his decisions were often questioned by analysts and industry observers. Rather than responding to criticism with reactionary decisions, he focused on proving the value of his strategy over time. His choice to stay the course, even as the firm's performance lagged and doubts grew, was a significant example of grit in action.
- **Seeing Long-Term Results and Continuing to Innovate:** Ultimately, James's transformation of Morgan Stanley was a years-long endeavor. Even after achieving measurable success, he continued to push for innovation within the wealth management division and set ambitious new goals. His willingness to continually refine and expand on his vision, rather than resting on the firm's early successes, further illustrates his grit and resilience..

Through these elements, James's leadership demonstrated that grit in the corporate world isn't just about taking bold actions but about the relentless pursuit of a challenging, sometimes uncertain path while weathering obstacles, criticism, and setbacks. James's legacy at Morgan Stanley reflects his endurance, adaptability, and steadfast commitment to long-term goals. His accomplishments are the culmination of his growth in early and mid-career, which equipped him to finish strong.

9

After the Summit

Building a Legacy through Social Capital

> One is too small a number to achieve greatness.
> —John C. Maxwell,
> *from The 17 Indisputable Laws of Teamwork*

I hope you understand that retirement is not a time of retreat. It is a moment of redefinition. For those who've spent decades climbing the mountain of professional accomplishment, the question can become "Who can I help climb next?" A great example of someone who embraced this post-peak phase with intentionality and influence is Louis V. Gerstner Jr.

In 1993, we started our company, Cornell International. We were a boot-strapping startup in the Hudson Valley of New York. That same year in the same Hudson Valley, a much, much bigger executive in a much, much bigger company was building his legacy by turning around IBM. When Gerstner took over IBM in 1993, the company faced what many believed was an existential crisis. Once a symbol of U.S. technological dominance, IBM was bleeding financially and struggling to adapt to a changing digital landscape. Gerstner wasn't a technologist; he was a strategist and systems thinker, and transformed the company by shifting its focus from hardware to integrated services and software. He famously broke with the corporate orthodoxy of the time, kept IBM intact when others called for its dismantling, and reestablished it as a leader in global enterprise services.

That turnaround, chronicled in his bestseller *Who Says Elephants Can't Dance?* (2003), was widely regarded as the pinnacle of a storied career. But what happened next was perhaps more instructive for leaders who seek to define life after the peak. Rather than slipping into a quiet retirement, Lou pivoted, moving from corporate savior to network builder, connector, and public advocate.

After stepping down from IBM in 2002, he became chairman of The Carlyle Group, one of the most influential private equity firms in the world. There, he applied his strategic insight to business investments and to build coalitions of global business leaders that helped shape capital flows and policy conversations, influencing multiple industries. He brought together networks of CEOs, investors, and policymakers—serving as a bridge between institutional knowledge and emerging leadership.

Lou didn't limit his post-peak engagement to only finance. He turned his focus to one of the most critical issues in U.S. society: public education. Through the Teaching Commission and later The Broad Center, Gerstner launched efforts to reform and reimagine K–12 leadership. Drawing on his extensive network, he mobilized executives, philanthropists, and policymakers to tackle systemic challenges in education—offering not just money, but strategic guidance and leadership development for school systems nationwide.

This was classic Lou Gerstner—not issuing commands, but building alliances. He understood that success in this next chapter of life would depend, not on his individual authority, but on his ability to bring people together around a shared mission. Throughout his post-CEO years, Gerstner was a writer, speaker, and mentor. He remained active on corporate boards and used his platform to challenge conventional thinking in business and public service. His relationships, carefully cultivated over decades, were not trophies—they were living assets. He activated those relationships to convene, to advise, and to empower others.

The lesson from Lou's post-peak career is clear: *The best leaders don't simply walk away after reaching the summit.* They descend with purpose, using their vantage point to help others climb. They turn influence into impact. And they understand that the real work of leadership—connecting people, shaping systems, and mentoring the next generation—may just be beginning.

You don't have to be a top Fortune 10 executive to apply the fundamentals of this playbook. If you retire as a plumber, deli-owner, taxi driver, mid-level manager, executive, or business owner, you have a network you can engage to assist and mentor the people who are on the way to their career peaks. Gerstner reminds us that a network is not what you build during your career to only achieve your peak—it's what you can draw on after your career to give back.

Inspiring Grit in Others: Teaching Others to Be Resilient and Disciplined

As someone climbs the career mountain, they gain much wisdom that can be shared. A leader's ability to inspire grit in others is one of the most valuable assets in building a resilient organization. When teams embody grit, they become more adaptable, motivated, and capable of handling challenges independently. Leaders who inspire grit cultivate a culture where resilience is celebrated, challenges are met with enthusiasm, and every team member feels empowered to contribute to the organization's success.

To pass on this wisdom, Admiral William H. McRaven, who led U.S. Special Operations Command, gave the commencement address at the University of Texas–Austin on May 17, 2014. He spoke about the lessons of resilience and discipline he learned during Navy SEAL training. He spoke about big challenges and small victories.

The admiral knows that to stay strong, a person has to focus on the small wins. Younger people in pursuit of their peak can benefit from this reminder. Victories may seem insignificant, but you must find them to endure the climb. They feed your resilience muscles. He emphasized the importance of something as simple as making your bed each morning as a small accomplishment that sets the tone for the day. He used this as a metaphor for the little victories of "getting things done" along the journey. As you mentor, remind people to focus on the small victories, like taking the next step toward a sale or getting moved up from a union apprentice to a union member, or they will likely burn out or lose stamina. Tell them it's okay to give themselves a pat on the back; it's fuel for the journey. This may sound simplistic, but it's a worthwhile exercise. Take the time to watch the McRaven's speech, available on YouTube. He shares his hard-won wisdom with the next generation.

This leader's message resonates far beyond the military because it highlights the idea that resilience is built through small, consistent actions that prepare us for larger challenges. Celebrating the small wins help maintain stamina. That's something many don't necessarily understand earlier in their careers. Sharing this message with others during your career peak can be very rewarding. Make it your business to do it.

As a leader during your peak phase, focus on setting an example of resilience. Share stories of overcoming challenges; celebrate the team's small wins; and emphasize the importance of persistence. Encourage team members to set stretch goals and approach setbacks as learning opportunities. Fostering a culture of resilience helps to create an environment where people are motivated to push through challenges and support each other.

Strategies for Cultivating the 5Qs in Others and Using Social Capital as a Peak-Level Leader

In the complex world of leadership, grit and social capital are indispensable tools for navigating challenges, building influence, and creating a positive impact. Table 9.1 lists some strategies to help you continue to cultivate these qualities in yourself and pass on to others.

Table 9.1 Strategies for Cultivating the 5Qs

Key Point	Description
Anchor Decisions in Core Values	When facing difficult choices, return to your core values. They are a compass to guide you through uncertainty and help you make decisions that align with your mission. Share this with your team.

Key Point	Description
Prioritize Authentic Relationships	Authenticity is the foundation of social capital. Make time to build genuine connections with your team, peers, and mentors. Approach each relationship with respect, empathy, and a willingness to support others.
Create a Culture of Transparency and Trust	Trust is essential for effective leadership. Foster a culture of transparency by being open about challenges, sharing information, and involving your team in decision-making. Trust strengthens your social capital and enhances your ability to lead through adversity. Be strong enough to be vulnerable; that is true leadership.
Embrace Feedback as a Tool for Growth	Leaders with grit are open to feedback and see it as an opportunity to improve. Encourage feedback from your team, peers, and mentors, and approach it with humility. Incorporating constructive feedback reinforces a culture of growth and resilience.
Develop Resilience Practices	Resilience isn't built overnight; it's developed through consistent habits. Engage in practices that strengthen mental and emotional resilience, like mindfulness, journaling, or regular exercise. These routines prepare you to face challenges with composure.
Mentor the Next Generation	Investing in others is one of the most powerful ways to extend your legacy. Make time to mentor, share your experiences, and encourage others to develop their grit and social capital. By supporting the growth of future leaders, you build a network of trust that continues to grow over time.

Conclusion: The Enduring Power of the 5Qs, Authenticity, and Social Capital in Leadership

At Korn Ferry our extensive research into leadership underscores the critical roles of grit and social capital in effective leadership. Our studies reveal that leaders who exhibit resilience and cultivate strong, trust-based relationships are better equipped to navigate challenges and drive organizational success.

Integrating Grit and Authenticity

Our company's findings suggest that the integration of grit and social capital is vital for leadership effectiveness. Leaders who demonstrate resilience while cultivating strong relationships are better positioned to inspire their teams and drive organizational success. This combination enables leaders to navigate complex challenges and adapt to changing environments.

In his book, *The Five Graces of Life and Leadership* (2021), Korn Ferry CEO Gary Burnison outlines five key traits—gratitude, resilience, aspiration, courage, and empathy—that collectively embody the essence of leadership grace. These traits align with the concepts of grit and social capital, and emphasize the importance of resilience and authentic relationships in effective leadership.

Korn Ferry research offers practical guidance for leaders aiming to enhance their grit and social capital. Here are a few highlights:

- **Self-awareness and development:** Leaders should assess their strengths and areas for growth, focusing on building resilience and emotional intelligence. This self-awareness enables them to navigate challenges effectively and build trust with their teams.
- **Authentic relationship building:** Investing time to develop genuine connections with team members and stakeholders fosters trust and collaboration and enhances social capital.
- **Inclusive leadership:** Create an environment that values and encourages diverse perspectives. This leads to innovation and strengthens a leader's social network.

- **Continuous learning:** Leaders committed to lifelong learning demonstrate grit and set an example for their teams, promoting a culture of growth and adaptability.

By embodying these practices, leaders can effectively integrate grit and social capital into their leadership approach, driving sustained success and fostering a positive organizational culture.

Effective leadership is not simply about authority. It's about resilience, influence, and the relationships built along the way. When someone cultivates grit, they equip themselves to lead through adversity, stay true to their vision, and inspire those around them. By building social capital, they create a foundation of trust and collaboration that amplifies their impact and fosters a culture of support.

As a leader, your legacy is defined not only by what you achieve, but also by the values and resilience you instill in others. Cultivating grit and social capital allows you to create a lasting impact that extends far beyond your tenure, and inspires others to lead with the same resilience, empathy, and integrity. In the end, the 5Qs and social capital are the ingredients of leadership that enable you to move forward and leave a positive mark on the world. These qualities enhance your leadership journey and contribute to a legacy that will endure long after you've moved on to new horizons.

Social Capital in Leadership

Social capital refers to the networks of relationships among individuals that facilitate cooperation and support. Korn Ferry research underscores the importance of leaders to build and leverage social capital to enhance their influence and effectiveness. Leaders who invest in authentic relationships create environments of trust and collaboration that leads to improved team performance and innovation.

10 | Sustaining Success through Continuous Growth and Adaptability

> Success breeds complacency. Complacency breeds failure. Only the paranoid survive.
>
> —Andy Grove, former CEO of Intel

Imagine it's the mid-1990s and you're Jeff Bezos, founder of Amazon. Your company, initially an online bookstore, has started to grow. But as you look around, you notice one pressing reality: If Amazon remains only a bookstore, it will eventually hit a ceiling. Instead of sticking with what worked initially, Bezos began to imagine what Amazon could become—a hub of e-commerce that would eventually expand to sell almost everything. That willingness to think big, adapt, and continuously seek new opportunities transformed Amazon into one of the most valuable companies in the world.

Continuous growth and adaptability aren't just desirable traits for companies; they're essential for individuals who seek sustained success. The ability to adapt and learn is about survival in an evolving world, and it's about thriving, pushing boundaries, and achieving new heights. Leaders and professionals who embrace change and seek growth redefine their fields, and leave lasting legacies. In this chapter, we'll explore how to sustain success by prioritizing continuous growth, nurturing adaptability, and maintaining resilience in the face of change.

Adapt to Change: Embrace a Flexible Mindset

Adaptability is one of the most critical skills for long-term success, especially in a world where technology, consumer expectations, and industries are constantly evolving. Those who adapt are better equipped to handle shifts, pivot strategies, and remain relevant.

Consider the story of Netflix, founded by Reed Hastings and Marc Randolph. Originally a DVD rental service, Netflix faced the same fate as other brick-and-mortar media companies as the internet began to change media consumption. Instead of sticking with their successful DVD model, Hastings and his team transitioned to streaming, an entirely new and, at the time, risky approach. Later, they embraced content creation that transformed Netflix into a media powerhouse. Each pivot required Netflix to let go of a successful model, adapt to new market demands, and redefine what it meant to entertain an audience. Today, Netflix is a leader in streaming and has fundamentally changed the way people consume media.

Let's look at Amazon again. In addition to transforming retail, Bezos has displayed remarkable grit and ingenuity with the development of Amazon Web Services (AWS), which grew to become a major revenue driver and a pioneering force in cloud computing. The story of AWS is a powerful illustration of how Jeff turned challenges into opportunities and showed a level of business flexibility and innovative thinking that went beyond Amazon's e-commerce roots.

The Birth of AWS: Identifying an Unexpected Opportunity

AWS began almost accidentally. In the early 2000s, Amazon's internal development teams struggled with a problem that few others had anticipated, the company's complex IT infrastructure. As Amazon expanded, its engineers frequently encountered bottlenecks and inefficiencies, which slowed development and impacted their ability to scale quickly. Each new project required a significant amount of custom infrastructure work, and the company was constantly reinventing the wheel to manage its own IT needs.

In a 2011 *Wired* interview, Bezos recounted the internal origin story clearly. He described the detailed conversations between engineers on the applications and infrastructure teams to improve their processes. These conversations happened daily, and Amazon engineers were looking for ways to make their internal systems more streamlined and reliable. As they started building tools to use at Amazon, they realized that there was tremendous demand for a platform to build web-scale applications from outside the company. Bezos realized, "With a little bit of extra work we could make it available to everybody. We're going to make it anyway—let's sell it." With this insight, AWS was born.

Building AWS Grit on an Unconventional Path

The launch of AWS was risky and, in many ways, an unconventional move. Amazon was known as an online retailer, not a technology provider. Shifting resources to build a cloud infrastructure platform was not an obvious or easy decision, especially when it required substantial capital investment and brought Amazon into direct competition with established tech giants like Microsoft and Google.

Many questioned the decision and saw it as a distraction from Amazon's core retail business. But Bezos remained focused on his vision. He believed that AWS had the potential to revolutionize how businesses operated and offered them scalable, affordable, and flexible infrastructure solutions. This persistence in pursuing AWS reflected his grit—the determination to forge ahead with an idea despite uncertainty and pushback. He was willing to take a significant risk, and believed AWS could redefine Amazon's future.

The Breakthrough of AWS Flexibility and Ingenuity

AWS officially launched in 2006 with just a handful of services, including Amazon S3 (Simple Storage Service) and EC2 (Elastic Compute Cloud). These services allowed customers to store and retrieve data and rent computing power on demand, paying only for the resources they used.

This pay-as-you-go model was revolutionary, disrupting traditional IT infrastructure that required companies to invest heavily in physical servers and data centers. I recently spoke to a top AWS executive who told me they now have more than 300 solutions and services from AWS and their partners.

The flexibility that AWS offered enabled startups and large companies to scale rapidly and cost effectively. Suddenly, businesses that once needed millions of dollars to build their IT infrastructure could do so with a credit card and a few clicks. This opened the door to innovation and enabled countless companies to experiment and grow in ways previously thought impossible.

Overcoming Setbacks on AWS's Path to Dominance

At the career peak, you are likely leading massive initiatives. They bring huge risks. The stakes are high. Your courage will be tested. Your resilience will be required. Your stamina must be there. This is how you win when you are at the peak.

Despite its potential, AWS faced many challenges in its early years. There were technical setbacks, security concerns, and significant skepticism from traditional IT providers. Initially, many companies were reluctant to trust Amazon with their data, especially given the sensitive nature of hosting proprietary information on someone else's servers.

AWS also encountered internal challenges. As it expanded, Amazon needed to create infrastructure for a new type of customer and provide tools for companies in diverse industries with unique requirements. The team encountered frequent technical roadblocks and had to innovate on the fly, developing solutions for issues that had never been encountered before in the tech industry.

Instead of retreating, Bezos' response to these challenges was to push AWS to deliver even better services. His grit came through in his insistence on constant improvement and relentless customer focus. Rather than seeing these setbacks as barriers, he viewed them as learning opportunities. His teams iterated on AWS's offerings until the platform became resilient, secure, and trusted by some of the world's largest corporations.

Achievements and Long-Term Impact: AWS Becomes Amazon's Growth Engine

Today, AWS is one of Amazon's most profitable divisions, generating more than $107 billion in revenue in 2024. It has become the world's leading cloud services provider, outpacing competitors like Microsoft Azure and Google Cloud. The success of AWS is a testament to its founder's foresight, flexibility, and commitment to innovation.

AWS fundamentally transformed Amazon's business model and turned the company from a retailer into a technology powerhouse. It allowed Amazon to diversify its revenue streams, stabilize the company's finances, and invest in other ventures like Prime, Alexa, and Amazon Studios. More broadly, AWS reshaped the tech landscape, and gave rise to the modern cloud computing industry that supports everything from small startups to global enterprises.

The Legacy of AWS: The Power of Grit and Innovation

The AWS story exemplifies a leader's willingness to take calculated risks, pursue ambitious ideas, and commit to a long-term vision despite challenges. Bezos' grit was essential to successfully launch AWS and maintain its trajectory of growth and continuous improvement. His work with AWS highlights the importance of flexibility and resilience in leadership and demonstrates that true innovation often involves ventures into unknown territory, setbacks as part of the journey, and the ability to maintain focus on a transformative vision.

Individuals and leaders who embrace adaptability must recognize that success requires change. Embrace the concept that change is a growth opportunity, not a disruption. This shift in mindset helps someone navigate new environments, learn new skills, and find new paths forward.

Ask yourself, "How can this change create new opportunities?" When you embrace change, potential setbacks become stepping stones for growth.

Build the Habit of Continuous Learning

In a world that never stops changing, staying relevant requires a commitment to lifelong learning. Leaders like Warren Buffett exemplify the value of constant growth. Even as one of the world's most successful investors, he dedicates hours each day to reading and learning, constantly refining his understanding of markets, businesses, and human behavior. His approach isn't just about gathering knowledge; it's about staying intellectually engaged and open to new insights.

For peak-career professionals, continuous learning prevents complacency and fosters the resilience to tackle challenges creatively. Learning doesn't have to be limited to your field of expertise. Engaging with new ideas, exploring diverse perspectives, and developing skills outside your core area of expertise all contribute to a more agile, adaptable mindset.

Lifelong Learning Embodied by Ron Moultrie

I got to know Ron Moultrie through a mutual friend, Jim McCann, founder of 1-800-Flowers. As a former military officer working in the career business, I am often asked to advise senior military officials on career planning, so Jim introduced me to Ron. It was instant friendship.

As the son of a Black U.S. Army soldier who enlisted in a segregated military, Moultrie's journey from a small New Jersey town to a career peak as U.S. Undersecretary of Defense illustrates the *Greatness Code* formula. Moultrie's distinguished career in U.S. intelligence and defense is a testament to the need for grit, social capital, and lifelong learning to succeed in your career.

While brilliance is not required for career success, being smart enough is. In Moultrie's case, he's brilliant, but that would not have been enough for him to rise in the ranks as he did. His drive and commitment to academic excellence have been lifelong passions and have helped level the playing field for a person of color. Moultrie's passion, resilience, and stamina fueled him to strive. He was voted most likely to succeed in his high school graduating class, was a military basic training honor graduate, and graduated magna cum laude from the University of Maryland. He obtained a Russian language degree from the Defense Language Institute at Monterey, California, a school with very few minority students. He was also a young leader in operational intelligence activities. He completed senior executive studies at Harvard University's Kennedy School of Government and earned a master's degree from the National Intelligence

Sustaining Success through Continuous Growth and Adaptability 127

University, a research university in Washington, DC. He also delivered its commencement address in 2024.

Lifelong learning takes stamina and passion. Moultrie's upbringing instilled in him a sense of strong work ethic, integrity, and a positivity that would serve him well in all facets of life. He began his public service in 1979 as a Russian linguist in the U.S. Air Force assigned to a remote base in Misawa, Japan. Unbeknownst to him, he was working for the super-secretive National Security Agency (NSA), where he would eventually begin a multi-decade career that culminated in his appointment as its director of operations. He was the first minority to serve in the role.

Moultrie told me that the NSA had few minorities in mission critical positions and even fewer in its most senior ranks early in his career. Arriving at the agency in 1983, he quickly found tiers among career fields, civilian and military members, and of course along racial lines. Realizing that there would be institutional and personality barriers, he committed to a formula that had already served him well: Be an extraordinary leader, who is highly competent and of the highest character. His efforts did not go unnoticed and put him on a trajectory to be the leader of the Department of Defense's intelligence and security enterprise.

Social capital also was critical to Moultrie's success. His network of colleagues, friends, and family encouraged and helped prepare him. His earliest supervisors and college professors encouraged him to keep his passion, drive, and what they deemed an "it" factor that could take him to the top.

Meeting, and eventually marrying, a fellow Russian linguist, Darlene, was a key moment. Although warned by a white supervisor that dating Darlene, who is white, would be detrimental to his career, they married. It led Moultrie to adopt an attitude that set him up to rise to the top and change the system from within. Although he worked hard for every promotion and accolade, he quickly deflects his success to mentors, champions, parents, colleagues, family, and what he deems the Lord's grace. Family prepared him for the realities of the world, while others provided opportunities for him to demonstrate his abilities.

He was asked to serve as a senior leader in the Central Intelligence Agency (CIA), a culture which Moultrie tells me is 180° from that at NSA;

his performance and reputation would later result in his selection as a member of CIA's Presidential Transition Team. On the national stage, Moultrie led NSA's review and assessment of the Naval Aircraft (EP-3) that made an emergency landing on Hainan Island China in 2001. He would later lead NSA's massive effort to review the Edward Snowden espionage incident. (Snowden leaked classified documents detailing NSA's massive surveillance operation, then fled to Russia to avoid prosecution.) As NSA's Deputy Operations Chief, Moultrie also played a key role in bringing al-Qaeda terrorist leader Osama Bin Laden to justice while also leading the world's most capable cyber organization.

Although decades earlier, the NSA had relegated minorities to working in the basement, Moultrie was given the agency's most challenging, high-profile assignments. His *firsts* would fill a separate book.

With exceptional resilience and determination, Moultrie overcame the challenges of prejudice that had driven some minorities to depart the agency. He told me, "Having to be a better performer, leader, problem solver and communicator, better educated and more experienced, and even a better dresser were the norm." Regardless, his goal was always to make it better for those that will follow.

Moultrie cites his nomination by President Biden to serve as undersecretary of defense for intelligence and security as the honor of a lifetime. In the post, he led the nation's 200,000 military intelligence and security professionals and oversaw a budget of approximately $30 billion dollar. As one of the Pentagon's top civilians, he was the key partner with the director of national intelligence on all intelligence and security matters and the principal advisor to the secretary of defense on these issues. He introduced a governance structure for the defense intelligence agencies to include the NSA, the Defense Intelligence Agency (DIA), the National Reconnaissance Office (NRO), the National Geospatial Agency (NGA), and the Defense Counterintelligence and Security Agency (DCSA) while simultaneously strengthening international bilateral and multilateral ties and alliances. He also advocated for greater collaboration with the private sector, more openness with the public, and the need to bring defense intelligence and security into the twenty-first century.

After Moultrie chose to leave his position as an undersecretary in February 2024, the president appointed him to the President's Intelligence Advisory Board (PIAB). He continued his public service on this distinguished board into 2025. He has received numerous accolades including the Presidential Rank Award; Department of Defense Medal for Distinguished Public Service; two National Intelligence Distinguished Service Medals; three NSA Exceptional Civilian Service Awards, the highest award conferred by the agency; induction into the Defense Language Institute/Foreign Language Center's Hall of Fame; the Department of Defense Meritorious Service for his military service; and a host of other awards and citations.

Moultrie's legacy is characterized by his steadfast commitment to national security, a lifelong desire of learning and service, and a drive to make any organization and its culture better. He has impeccable integrity and represents what's best about our nation. A true inspiration, he personifies how grit, resilience, partnerships, and dedication shape the most successful high achievers. His ability to continually learn to keep up with both political dynamics and sophisticated technology advancements was key to his success.

To build a habit of continuous learning, set aside dedicated time for it each day or week. That learning could include reading books, taking online courses, attending workshops, or networking with individuals outside your field. The more you learn, the more you expand your ability to adapt to new challenges and remain effective in an ever-changing landscape.

The Role of Self-Reflection in Sustaining Growth

Continuous growth is about external learning and internal development. Self-reflection is a powerful tool to help you recognize areas for improvement, understand personal strengths, and gain clarity on your goals. Leaders who prioritize self-reflection maintain a keen awareness of their values and priorities, which helps them navigate both successes and setbacks with a grounded perspective.

Again, consider the example of Bill Gates, who has a habit of taking *think weeks*—a time away from work to read, reflect, and explore ideas without distractions. This practice allows him to evaluate his goals, consider new ideas, and return to work with renewed focus and insight. For him, self-reflection has been a key element in sustaining his success and broadening his impact.

To incorporate self-reflection into your routine, set aside regular intervals to evaluate your performance, goals, and areas for growth. Journaling, meditation, or even quiet walks can provide the space needed to reflect deeply on your personal and professional journey. This habit not only fosters self-awareness, but also ensures that your growth aligns with your core values and long-term goals.

Embrace a Growth Mindset: View Challenges as Opportunities

A growth mindset—the belief that abilities and intelligence can be developed through effort—is critical to sustain success. Leaders with a growth mindset are more resilient in the face of setbacks and see challenges as opportunities to learn and improve. Carol Dweck coined the term *growth mindset*, explaining that this perspective helps individuals thrive, especially during difficult times.

For professionals, a growth mindset involves reframing setbacks as valuable feedback. Instead of perceiving a challenge as an obstacle, it becomes a chance to expand your skills and deepen your understanding. Embrace curiosity in every situation. Ask questions like "What can I learn from this?" or "How can this make me better?" When you adopt a growth mindset, you will cultivate the resilience needed to thrive, even when faced with significant challenges.

Develop Adaptability in Your Team: Foster a Culture of Growth

Adaptability is essential not only for individual success, but also for team and organizational resilience. Leaders who prioritize adaptability create environments where team members feel empowered to innovate, learn, and grow. An adaptable team is better equipped to handle disruptions, pivot strategies, and remain competitive in a changing landscape.

Consider Xavier Rolet. He was my client for nine years. I would meet with him every time I went to London. During each visit, I felt as though I was getting a PhD in financial market structure and business strategy. He took the helm as CEO of the London Stock Exchange Group in 2009, and set out to reinvent the institution. During his near-nine-year tenure, Rolet pursued an aggressive acquisition strategy - adding MillenniumIT (2009), Turquoise (2010), FTSE Group (2011), LCH.Clearnet (2013), the Frank Russell Company (2014), among others—which expanded the Group's footprint from trading to clearing, to indices, and tech services. He championed the "Open Access" model—later embedded EU MiFIR regulation—which broke down traditional vertical silos and allowed clients to mix and match venue, clearing, and data services.

Perhaps most strikingly, under his tenure, the market valuation of the London Stock Exchange Group surged.

Rolet's vision transformed the LSE, but his grit made it happen. Along the way, he faced countless challenges from competitors and regulators. It was a nine year climb, fueled by stamina, persistence, and resilience.

Maintain Resilience through Change

Change, even positive change, can be a challenge. Leaders who succeed in the long term know how to stay resilient in the face of disruption. Resilience is the ability to adapt to change without losing focus on one's goals and values. It involves managing stress, maintaining optimism, and using challenges as opportunities for growth.

One example of resilience in the face of change is Indra Nooyi, former CEO of PepsiCo. When Nooyi took the helm, she initiated a strategic pivot, and focused on healthier products to align with the evolution of consumer preferences. This transition faced pushback from shareholders and employees who were accustomed to PepsiCo's traditional business model. Yet,

Nooyi's resilience, combined with her ability to communicate her vision, allowed her to navigate the challenges and lead PepsiCo through a successful transformation.

To cultivate resilience, start by building practices that help you manage stress and maintain perspective. Exercise, meditation, and maintain a strong support network to help you stay balanced. Additionally, embrace the idea that change, though challenging, often leads to growth and new opportunities. By viewing change as a catalyst for improvement, you'll strengthen your ability to lead through transitions.

Build a Legacy of Growth and Adaptability—CEOs at Their Peak

At the peak of your career, one of the most rewarding aspects of growth and adaptability is the opportunity to build a legacy. A legacy goes beyond personal success; it's about the positive impact you leave on others and the contributions you make to your field. Leaders who prioritize growth and adaptability inspire those around them and create a ripple effect that extends beyond their own careers.

Consider the legacy of Steve Jobs, co-founder of Apple. Jobs' adaptability and commitment to growth led him to develop products that redefined technology and culture. Even after his death, his willingness to pivot, learn, and innovate continues to influence Apple and the tech industry as a whole. Jobs' legacy is a testament to the power of continuous growth and adaptability, and inspires future generations to pursue excellence and embrace change.

My colleagues at Korn Ferry, Jane Edison Stevenson and Evelyn Orr, conducted an important study into the progression of women to the ranks of CEOs.

On International Women's Day in 2018, Korn Ferry republished some of Jane and Evelyn's key findings on gender diversity and developing women leaders from the original article, "What Makes Women CEOs Different?"

The following is an excerpt.

"March to Equality: Advancing Women Worldwide." Women CEOs' ranks are still far below what they should be, and change continues to come slowly. But a landmark study by Korn Ferry has pinpointed the critical traits that are landing women in the rarified world of becoming a CEO.

According to the study, women CEOs are slightly older than their male counterparts, in part because it takes them 30 percent longer than men to reach the corner office. But those who reached the top were often committed to making profound changes at their organizations.

The four-month research offers a rare glimpse at how female CEOs operate. Some 57 women CEOs—from 41 Fortune 1,000 companies and 16 large privately held companies—were interviewed and given detailed assessments over the spring and summer. The work was supported by a grant from The Rockefeller Foundation as part of its "100×25" initiative, which aims to support the hiring of 100 Fortune 500 women CEOs by 2025.

"Given there had been only 94 women CEOs ever in the Fortune 500, at the time of the study we were thrilled at the high participation rate," said Stevenson, Korn Ferry's global leader for CEO succession, who led the groundbreaking research initiative. "Rather than focusing on why more women are not CEOs, we focused on quantifying what their common success factors were: experiences, competencies, traits, and drivers that enabled them to become CEO of a major company. Understanding these remarkably consistent key indicators of women's potential and, in turn, redefining needed organizational impact factors, can help change the game for both organizations and the women who will lead them."

As part of the interviews, the CEOs were asked to discuss a range of topics, including their personal histories, careers, and key personality traits and drivers. Many also completed Korn Ferry's own executive assessment.

(continued)

(continued)

In all, six key insights emerged with surprising consistency across all the women CEOs who participated in the study:

1. **These CEOs worked harder and longer to get to the top.** The women CEOs were an average of four years older than their male counterparts and worked in a slightly greater number of roles, functions, companies, and industries.
2. **They were driven by both a sense of purpose and achieving business results.** More than two-thirds of the women interviewed and assessed said they were motivated by a sense of purpose and their belief that their company could have a positive impact on the community, employees, and the world around them. Nearly a quarter pointed to creating a positive culture as one of their proudest accomplishments.
3. **Differentiating traits sustained the women's success on the road to CEO.** Defining traits and competencies that emerged time and again in the research included courage, risk-taking, resilience, agility, and managing ambiguity.
4. **They were more likely to engage the power of teams.** Women CEOs scored significantly higher than the benchmark group on humility—indicative of a consistent lack of self-promotion, an expressed appreciation for others, and a tendency to share the credit—and were more likely to leverage others to achieve desired results.
5. **Despite evident potential, the women didn't generally set their sights on becoming a CEO.** Two-thirds of the women said they never realized they could become CEO until a boss or mentor encouraged them, and instead, focused on hitting business targets and seeking new challenges rather than on their personal career advancement.
6. **The women shared STEM and financial backgrounds that served as a springboard.** Early in their careers, nearly 60 percent of the women had demonstrable expertise in either STEM

Sustaining Success through Continuous Growth and Adaptability

(40 percent) or business/finance/economics (19 percent)—all fields where they could prove themselves with precise, definable outcomes, and also ones crucial to success of the business.

The research report recommends clear steps that companies can take to accelerate and maintain a steady supply of women CEO candidates, including early identification of high-potential talent and communicating opportunities in terms that play to women's strengths and engage specific drivers. Mentors also play an indispensable role, affirming potential to encourage more women to strive to become CEOs and, later on, sponsors can actively help advance women's careers. These recommendations are currently being applied to design specific programs for a list of beta companies eager to produce more women leaders.

"One thing that struck us during the research was how closely the women CEOs' traits aligned with those of the modern leaders that boards are now seeking: courageous and able to successfully navigate uncertainty and ambiguity in a constantly shifting environment," said Orr, chief operating officer of the Korn Ferry Institute and a leader of the research initiative. "While The Rockefeller Foundation's '100×25' initiative is an ambitious one, we are convinced that, as more organizations experience the positive business results of tapping women in the CEO pipeline, additional companies will follow suit."

These CEO's made their way to the top by their own initiative and their networks. They support the future generations as they pursue their Greatness Objectives. They have lessons to teach from experience.

To build a legacy of growth, focus on empowering others to develop adaptability and a commitment to learning. Mentor future leaders, share your insights, and encourage a mindset of continuous improvement. By fostering a culture of growth, you create a lasting impact that endures beyond your tenure, influencing others to lead with resilience and adaptability.

One quote from the original article published in the *Harvard Business Review* is telling:

> Throughout the study's assessments of female CEOs, a combination of four traits and competencies emerged as key to their success: courage, risk-taking, resilience, and managing ambiguity. As one woman told us, "When I went down to Atlanta to run that market for the company, the president of the division said, 'You are going to be fired within a year, because no one has been able to make Atlanta successful'. I went anyhow."

While this study was published in 2018, the insights demonstrate that the 5Qs were clearly key components of the career success formula for these executives in the two to three decades that preceded their peaks.

The Enduring Power of Growth and Adaptability

Friends and colleagues who know me well agree that I've been at Korn Ferry for five years; three-times in a row. It is a recognition that in my first 15 years with the company, I seemed to get bored and needed a new challenge, every five years. Fortunately, our company is very flexible and we were always able to reinvent me within the company. The company provided new challenges and opportunities to grow.

To sustain success requires more than reaching the top; it demands a commitment to continuous growth and adaptability. Leaders who embrace change, prioritize learning, and cultivate resilience are better prepared to navigate the complexities of a dynamic world. When someone fosters a growth mindset and empowers those around them to embrace adaptability, they build a legacy of excellence, resilience, and positive impact.

As you reflect on your journey, remember that the pursuit of growth and adaptability is an ongoing process. Each challenge, transition, and success contributes to a career defined not only by personal achievements but by a lasting influence on others. Through continuous growth and adaptability, you can lead with purpose, inspire change, and create a legacy that endures beyond your own career (See Table 10.1).

Table 10.1 Strategies for Sustaining Growth and Adaptability

Practice	Description
Anchor Decisions in Core Values	When facing difficult choices, return to your core values. Clear values serve as a compass, guide you through uncertainty, and help you make decisions that align with your mission.
Prioritize Authentic Relationships	Authenticity is the foundation of social capital. Make time to build genuine connections with your team, peers, and mentors. Approach each relationship with respect, empathy, and a willingness to support others.
Create a Culture of Transparency and Trust	Trust is essential for effective leadership. Foster a culture of transparency by being open about challenges, sharing information, and involving your team in decision-making. Trust strengthens your social capital and enhances your ability to lead through adversity.
Embrace Feedback as a Tool for Growth	Leaders with grit are open to feedback, view it as an opportunity to improve. Encourage feedback from your team, peers, and mentors, and approach it with humility. Incorporating constructive feedback reinforces a culture of growth and resilience.
Develop Resilience Practices	Resilience isn't built overnight; it's developed through consistent habits. Engage in practices that strengthen mental and emotional resilience like mindfulness, journaling, or regular exercise. These routines prepare you to face challenges with composure.
Mentor the Next Generation	Investing in others is one of the most powerful ways to extend your legacy. Make time to mentor, share your experiences, and encourage others to develop their grit and social capital. By supporting the growth of future leaders, you build a network of trust that continues to grow over time.

11

The Power of a Legacy Defined by Grit and Social Capital

> Carve your name on hearts, not tombstones. A legacy is etched into the minds of others and the stories they share about you.
> —Shannon L. Alder author of *300 Questions to Ask Your Parents Before It's Too Late*

Once again I look to the story of Supreme Court Justice Ruth Bader Ginsburg. Known affectionately as the Notorious RBG, Ginsburg's legacy is woven into the fabric of U.S. history, a testament to her grit and unwavering commitment to justice and equality. Through decades of advocacy, she fought against gender discrimination, pushed boundaries, and challenged the status quo. But Ginsburg's influence wasn't solely based on her legal acumen. Her lasting legacy also was shaped by the relationships she built, even with those who opposed her views. Her respectful relationship with fellow Justice Antonin Scalia, for example, despite their ideological differences, is a testament to her belief in the value of social capital.

In the later stages of a career, the question of legacy becomes paramount. Legacy isn't just about individual accomplishments; it's about the values and influence that endure beyond your tenure. Leaders who understand the importance of grit and social capital leave behind more than results—they leave a culture of resilience, collaboration, and positive impact. In this chapter, we'll explore how to cultivate a legacy that reflects the principles of grit and social capital, influencing future generations and building a lasting impact that extends well beyond your professional achievements.

Define Your Legacy: The Role of Grit and Social Capital

The concept of legacy often evokes thoughts of accolades, achievements, or financial wealth, but a true legacy is about more than these visible markers. It's about the intangible values, principles, and relationships you leave behind. Leaders who incorporate grit and social capital into their lives create legacies that are resilient, inclusive, and deeply impactful.

To define your own legacy, reflect on the values you hold most dear. What principles do you want to impart to others? What impact do you want to have on your field, community, or society at large? When your actions align with these values and focus on building positive relationships, you begin to shape a legacy grounded in both grit and social capital.

Lead by Example: Inspire Grit in Others

One of the most powerful ways to leave a legacy is to inspire others to develop their own resilience. Leaders who model grit—face challenges head-on, learn from failures, and pursue goals with unwavering determination—create a culture that values persistence and strength. This culture of resilience can influence team members, mentees, and colleagues, and empower them to overcome obstacles in their own careers.

Build Strong Connections: The Foundation of Social Capital in Legacy

Social capital—the network of relationships built on trust, mutual respect, and collaboration—is a foundational element of a lasting legacy. Leaders who invest in building strong connections create environments where others feel valued, supported, and inspired to contribute. When you foster relationships that transcend transactional interactions, you build a legacy that reflects the power of connection.

Clifford Alexander: A Legacy of Passion, Resilience, and Leadership

I offer Clifford Alexander Jr. as a great example. He was the Secretary of the Army while I was enrolled as a cadet at West Point. Years later, I had the honor of collaborating with him while he served on the board of directors of Mutual of America Financial Group.

One of Alexander's greatest strengths was his ability to cultivate relationships. Throughout his career, he mentored young Black leaders, ensuring that the doors he opened remained open for others. His network included influential politicians, business leaders, and activists, all of whom recognized his ability to drive meaningful change.

Even after he left public office, he remained active in advocacy, law, and business. He served as a consultant advising on corporate diversity and inclusion efforts. His ability to navigate both public and private sectors demonstrated his adaptability and deep understanding of leadership dynamics. The secretary was a man of immense determination. He navigated the corridors of power and broke barriers with relentless passion. Born in 1933 in New York City to working-class parents, he grew up in an America where racial discrimination was deeply ingrained. From a young age, he learned the value of perseverance and the importance of building strong alliances to achieve success. His journey from Harlem to the highest echelons of government serves as a testament to grit, resilience, and the power of a well-cultivated network.

Early Challenges Overcoming Barriers

Growing up in the 1940s, he encountered systemic racism that sought to limit his potential. Yet, he remained undeterred. His parents instilled in him the belief that education was the gateway to opportunity. With their encouragement, he excelled academically, earning a place at Harvard University.

As one of the few Black students in his class, he faced prejudice, but leveraged his intellect and charisma to build meaningful connections. Harvard was not just an education—it was a training ground for leadership, and taught him the importance of networks and advocacy. He graduated in 1955, then pursued a law degree at Yale, further sharpening his legal and strategic acumen.

Forging a Path in Public Service

After completing his education, the future secretary of the Army entered the legal and political arenas. It was a time when opportunities for African Americans in government were scarce. He started in the White House as a National Security Council officer under President John F. Kennedy. This opportunity provided him with firsthand experience in policymaking and access to influential figures.

His talent did not go unnoticed. Under the next presidential administration, that of Lyndon B. Johnson, he was appointed the first Black chairman of the Equal Employment Opportunity Commission (EEOC). In this role, he fought tirelessly for workplace equality, ensuring that marginalized communities had a fair chance at employment and improving diversity in military leadership ranks. His ability to navigate political landscapes and push for change exemplified his resilience.

A History Maker

In 1977, President Jimmy Carter appointed Alexander the first Black secretary of the Army. This historic appointment was not merely symbolic; the new secretary understood that representation at the top was crucial to inspire future generations. Despite resistance from those who opposed his progressive policies, he remained steadfast. He built alliances within the military and the government, ensuring that his reforms had lasting impact. His ability to connect with people across different spectrums of influence played a key role in his success.

A Legacy of Tenacity and Impact

Clifford Alexander's life is a master class in resilience, passion, and the power of networking. His story teaches us that success is more than personal ambition—it's about lifting others along the way. From breaking racial barriers to implementing lasting reforms, he exemplified what it means to persevere against the odds.

His journey serves as an enduring reminder that resilience and relationships can transform not only one's own life but the lives of many. He climbed the ladder of success, and held it steady for others to ascend.

To build strong connections that contribute to your legacy, prioritize authenticity in your interactions. Invest time understanding others' perspectives, show empathy, and offer support. Seek to understand, listen without judgment, and create a culture of inclusivity. These relationships form the foundation of a legacy rooted in social capital, one that endures because of the genuine bonds you've fostered.

Pass the Torch: Mentorship and Knowledge Sharing

Mentorship is one of the most powerful ways to extend your legacy. When you mentor others, you pass on skills, insights, values, and principles that define your approach to success. Mentorship fosters continuity and allows your impact to live on through the achievements and growth of those you've guided.

Additionally, the stories of poet Maya Angelou and media mogul Oprah Winfrey exemplify the profound impact of mentorship. An Instagram post attributed to Winfrey says, "I've been blessed to have Maya Angelou as my mentor, mother/sister, and friend since my 20's. She was there for me always, guiding me through some of the most important years of my life. The world knows her as a poet but at the heart of her, she was a teacher. 'When you learn, teach. When you get, give' is one of my best lessons from her. That mentorship shaped Oprah's approach to life, career, and philanthropy, and created a legacy that lives on through her work and the lives she continues to impact.

To create a legacy through mentorship, seek out opportunities to support and guide others. Share not only your knowledge but also the lessons you've learned from your experiences, including challenges and failures.

Encourage mentees to develop their own resilience, social capital, and unique strengths. By investing in the growth of others, you extend your influence and create a legacy that lives on in the success and character of future leaders.

Create a Culture of Collaboration and Trust

A lasting legacy often involves the creation of a culture that embodies your values. Leaders who foster a collaborative, inclusive, and trusting environment don't just leave behind results; they leave a culture that continues to inspire, support, and empower others long after they've moved on.

Indra Nooyi, who I first mentioned in Chapter 10, exemplified this approach as the CEO at PepsiCo. During her tenure, she emphasized the importance of empathy, inclusivity, and innovation, and created a culture where employees felt valued and inspired to contribute. Her commitment to diversity and social responsibility shaped PepsiCo's culture, and influenced not only its business practices but also the broader corporate world. Today, her legacy is reflected in PepsiCo's ongoing commitment to these values and illustrates the enduring impact of a culture built on respect, trust, and collaboration.

To build a legacy through culture, lead by example, and make your values visible in your actions. Foster an environment where diverse perspectives are welcomed, where collaboration is encouraged, and where individuals feel safe to take risks and innovate. A culture grounded in these values becomes a lasting part of a legacy, and inspires future leaders to uphold and build on the principles you've established.

The Impact of Ethical Leadership on Legacy

Ethical leadership—making decisions that align with principles of fairness, integrity, and respect—plays a significant role in shaping a positive legacy. Leaders who prioritize ethical behavior create a foundation of trust and respect that resonates long after their tenure. Ethical leadership defines individual reputations and also sets standards that influence organizational practices, industry norms, and even societal values.

An exemplary case of ethical leadership is that of Paul Polman, former CEO of Unilever, the London-based multinational consumer packaged goods company. Polman was known for his commitment to sustainable business practices, and his pursuit of long-term goals over short-term profits. Under his leadership, Unilever adopted a sustainability-focused approach that championed environmental responsibility and social impact. Polman's ethical stance influenced Unilever's culture and positioned the company as a leader in corporate responsibility and an inspiration for other organizations to prioritize sustainability. His legacy reflects the profound impact of ethical leadership on both company and industry standards.

To build a legacy grounded in ethics, consistently align your decisions with your values. Be transparent, hold yourself accountable, and prioritize integrity in every interaction. Encourage ethical behavior in your organization and set standards that reflect respect for both individuals and the broader community. Ethical leadership creates a legacy of trust and respect, and establishes a foundation on which future leaders can build.

Measuring the Impact of Your Legacy

Legacy is difficult to quantify, but its impact can be observed through the lives you've touched, the values you've instilled, and the changes you've inspired. Leaders who focus on building a legacy of grit and social capital often see their influence ripple through others' achievements, the culture they've created, and the positive impact on their industry or community.

For example, Martin Luther King, Jr.'s legacy endures through the countless individuals he inspired to continue advocating for civil rights, equality, and justice. His grit, vision, and unwavering commitment to peaceful change set a standard that continues to influence leaders, activists, and citizens around the world. King's legacy isn't measured in titles or accolades but in the ongoing movement for justice that he helped ignite.

To measure the impact of your legacy, look at the people, culture, and values you've influenced. Consider the mentorships you've fostered; the cultural changes you've implemented; and the individuals who have been inspired by your example. A legacy rooted in grit and social capital leaves an enduring mark, seen in the resilience, unity, and shared values that persist long after your direct involvement. See Table 11.1.

Table 11.1 Strategies for Building a Lasting Legacy

Practice	Description
Define your Core Values	Start by identifying the values that matter most to you. These values should guide your decisions, actions, and relationships, and ensure that your legacy aligns with what you stand for.
Lead with Integrity	Ethical leadership is the cornerstone of a respected legacy. Consistently make decisions that align with principles of fairness, respect, and integrity. Transparency and accountability create a foundation of trust that endures.
Invest in Relationships	Social capital is a lasting part of your legacy. Build meaningful connections based on empathy, respect, and support. These relationships create a network of trust that extends beyond your immediate influence.
Mentor Future Leaders	Mentorship allows you to pass on knowledge, values, and resilience. By guiding others, you empower them to carry your legacy forward through their own achievements.
Foster a Positive Culture	Create a culture that reflects your values, prioritizing collaboration, inclusivity, and trust. A strong culture becomes a part of your legacy, and inspires future leaders to uphold and expand on your principles.
Embrace Adaptability and Growth	A lasting legacy is one that adapts to change. Show resilience in the face of challenges, embrace new ideas, and encourage others to pursue growth and improvement.

Facing Reality: You May Never Become the CEO—Good For You!

When professionals join organizations, many have the ambition to become the boss. Over a period of years, many decide they don't want that next big job or, sadly, many are passed over for that next big job they coveted.

Eventually, they just know they probably won't rise much higher in their business careers, or they simply decide they want to broaden their focus beyond their day job.

There are countless examples of people who peaked at career levels below what they aspired to. They found a way to be okay with that, and they took their skills and experiences to other venues while still working. They become school board members. They start small side-hustle businesses. They join civic organizations. In these new endeavors, while still working, they can possibly rise to prominence. They peaked at work and pivoted to something new in their free time. They are now in a new realm where rising to a top leadership role may be within their grasp.

The key takeaway? The skills that get you to where you are, can be repurposed for where you want to go in a new venue. You can find achievement and satisfaction, and add to your fulfillment by pursuing other activities while still working in your day job. You can find a new venue where your leadership can be appreciated.

Pivot toward Purpose: Explore Career, Community, and Calling

Think about this hypothetical example: It's a Tuesday morning when Jonathan realizes he has peaked. He's at his desk in a career where he has spent three decades climbing a corporate ladder, and he's staring at his reflection in the dark screen of his laptop. Jonathan always imagined he'd end up in the C-suite, but here he was, a senior manager, well-compensated and respected, but undeniably stuck. It wasn't failure, exactly. But it wasn't what he'd dreamed of either.

In his book, *Outliers: The Story of Success* (2008), Malcolm Gladwell explores the intersection of opportunity and success. Success, he argues, is often about seizing the opportunities others don't see. But what happens when you're no longer chasing a summit, and are standing on a plateau? That's where the pivot comes in—a redirection of talent, experience, and ambition toward something new. In Jonathan's case, he decided to leverage his professional skills to serve his community. Within a year, he was chairman of the board of a local nonprofit and leading a mentorship program for at-risk youth. His career hadn't ended; it had transformed. See Table 11.2.

Table 11.2 Practical Steps to Pivot

Steps	Details
Redefine your Metrics of Success	Ask yourself: What does success mean to me now? For Jonathan, it was no longer about title or income but about impact and perhaps a new venue to rise to top leadership.
Leverage your Network	Much like Gladwell's concept of the tipping point, your network can be a catalyst for change. Reach out to mentors, colleagues, and friends already engaged in meaningful work. They may open doors you never knew existed.
Start Small but Start Now	Whether you volunteer on weekends, join a nonprofit board, or attend a local government meeting, small steps can help you test the waters before making a larger commitment.
Seek out Stories for Inspiration	Immerse yourself in the narratives of others who have successfully pivoted. These stories provide guidance and also reinforce the idea that reinvention is possible at any stage of life.

The insight here is that success is rarely a straight line. It's a series of jagged paths, each with its own opportunities for reinvention. I have found that individuals who shift their focus to community-based or charitable work often tell me they are more fulfilled than when they were working for a paycheck.

Lessons from Real-Life Pivots

Three key maxims to follow include:

1. **Build on your skills, not your title:** John Wood was a Microsoft executive on the rise, but a vacation to Nepal changed everything. While trekking through rural villages, he visited a school where children had no books. This experience inspired him to leave his corporate career and found Room to Read, an organization

that has since built libraries in thousands of underprivileged communities. Wood's pivot wasn't a rejection of his corporate skills but a redirection of them. He leveraged his business acumen to create a global movement.

Gladwell might liken Wood's story to that of an entrepreneur who sees a unique gap in the market—in this case, a gap in societal needs rather than consumer goods. The key takeaway? The skills that get you to where you are can be repurposed for where you want to go.

2. **Find a community that inspires you:** Take the example of Jessica Jackley, co-founder of Kiva Microfunds, a San Francisco–based nonprofit that specializes in microfinancing. She had always been passionate about addressing poverty, but found herself working in a traditional nonprofit job that felt stagnant. Inspired by microfinance success stories in developing countries, she pivoted her focus and co-created a platform that allowed people to lend directly to entrepreneurs in need. Her story is a reminder that community work doesn't have to fit a predefined mold. Sometimes, the most impactful contributions come from creating something new.

    Jessica's pivot was a *connector moment*—one where an individual's experience intersects with a network of others who share their vision, creating a ripple effect far greater than any one person could achieve alone.

3. **Embrace the power of faith and purpose:** My work with the Capuchin Franciscan's Province of Saint Mary has shown me that many people discover that their second act after a primary career is well lived through service rooted in faith. By embracing the power of faith and purpose, they find new meaning in ministry, community outreach, or spiritual leadership. This path often provides not only renewal for themselves but also lasting impact for others.

    Faith-based pivots often resonate deeply with those who seek purpose; research supports their impact. A study published in *Social Science & Medicine* found that individuals who engage in religious or spiritual volunteering report higher levels of well-being and resilience, particularly during life transitions.

The Freedom to Choose Impact

In Gladwell's world, success often hinges on recognizing moments of opportunity that others overlook. Pivoting your career toward community, charitable, or faith-based work is one such moment—a chance to reframe what fulfillment looks like and to leave a legacy that extends beyond professional achievements.

Our hypothetical Jonathan, for his part, now spends his days mentoring young leaders and designing community initiatives. He no longer measures success by promotions or paychecks. Instead, he counts it in lives touched and futures changed. And in this new chapter, he's found something he never quite had at the peak of his corporate climb: peace.

Conclusion: The Enduring Impact of a Legacy Built on Grit and Social Capital

A legacy built on grit and social capital extends beyond individual accomplishments. It's about the influence you leave on others, the values you instill, and the positive changes you inspire. Leaders who prioritize resilience, build authentic connections, and lead with integrity create legacies that endure and impact both individuals and communities.

As you consider your own legacy, remember that each act of perseverance, each relationship built, and each ethical decision contribute to a lasting impact. When you embrace grit and nurture Social Capital, you create a legacy that reflects the best of your character, and inspires others to lead with the same strength, empathy, and commitment.

In the end, a legacy grounded in grit and social capital is one that lives on through the people you've touched, the values you've championed, and the positive influence you've shared with the world. This legacy defines your career and enriches the lives of those who carry it forward to create a ripple effect that extends across generations.

12 | The Balance of Grit and Well-Being

> We think, mistakenly, that success is the result of the amount of time we put in at work, instead of the quality of time we put in.
> We sacrifice our health and our relationships for our drive, and we forget that we're not machines.
>
> —Arianna Huffington

I coach highly driven people. They can't fathom the notion of falling short. However, they all do on occasion. That's when I tell them, "you ARE NOT invincible – take a pause." When we think of grit, we often picture the relentless pursuit of goals, an unyielding drive to overcome obstacles, and a laser focus on the achievement of success. And while grit is indeed essential for long-term achievement, it can sometimes overshadow an equally crucial aspect of sustained success: well-being. Grit, when exercised without balance, can lead to burnout, diminished mental and physical health, and even undermine the very goals it's meant to support. When I coach junior leaders and executives, I remind them they are not invincible. When you feel tired or hit a wall, it's okay. Take a break. Catch your breath. Enjoy the short pause and then move ahead. I often use this phrase to make my point: "You have to slow down to go fast." I really mean it. Moving too fast can put you out of control and heading for a crash.

Arianna Huffington, founder of *The Huffington Post*, is driven by her passion for success. In the beginning, she worked tirelessly and often sacrificed sleep and well-being to reach her goals. One day, she collapsed and woke up with a fractured cheekbone and cuts over her eye. The doctors determined the cause was exhaustion. This wake-up call forced her to confront the reality of her lifestyle. She realized that while grit and hard work had contributed to her success, they weren't sustainable without a commitment to self-care. Huffington went on to become an advocate for well-being in the workplace, recognizing that success must be balanced with health and wellness to be truly sustainable.

I had the opportunity to interview Barbara Corcoran years ago. At that time, her website (www.BarbaraCorcoran.com) had an "About Me" section, which appeared in my book *Smart Is Not Enough* (Wiley, 2007). She clearly built her career on the 5Qs and social capital. Her journey was a tough one, beginning in elementary school.

When you read Barbara Corcoran's writings, she says that her credentials included straight D's in high school and college and 20 jobs by the time she turned 23. But it was her next job that would make her one of the most successful entrepreneurs in the country, when she borrowed $1,000 from her boyfriend and quit her job as a waitress to start a tiny real estate company in New York City. Over the next 25 years, she'd parlay that $1,000 loan into a multi-billion real estate business, which she sold for millions of dollars and then began a second career helping business founders for her next chapter.

When I interviewed Barbara back then, it was to get her perspective on my South Pole Theory. We discussed her experiences in school and at work in great detail. In the book, I note five key attributes that distinguish people who haven't been exceptional academic performers, yet emerge years later as high achievers in their fields. I sum up the five attributes this way: They are strong *communicators*, they have experienced *suffering or extreme challenges*, they somehow *always stood out*, they *had passion*, and they were *notably creative*.

Barbara clearly achieved her Greatness Objective and moved on to a second career, which led to fame with the *Shark Tank* TV show and as an investor. Importantly, Barbara also learned the importance of balancing grit with well-being. She has spoken openly about the times when her relentless drive would wear her down. In her early career, as she built her real estate business from scratch, she pushed herself to the limit, often working seven days a week and juggling immense stress. But over time, she realized that to stay resilient and creative, she needed to prioritize her mental and physical health. So, Barbara developed a habit of integrating personal wellness into her routine, such as taking regular breaks to reset, practicing gratitude, and even using humor to manage stress. Her commitment to well-being allowed her to approach challenges with renewed energy, ultimately helping her build a lasting legacy in business. However, Barbara is also the ultimate realist. In *Inc.*, Diana Ransom quoted Barbara as saying, "I gave up on balance (in life) a long time ago." Now, she says, "I strive for anti-exhaustion."

Remember: You are not invincible, and sometimes work will be the priority. Other times, it will need to take a back seat. How you manage this is the key.

Understand Burnout: The Consequences of Unbalanced Grit

Burnout is a state of chronic stress that arises when individuals push themselves beyond their limits for extended periods. Driven by a sense of obligation, desire to achieve, or sheer perseverance, people with high grit can sometimes ignore early signs of burnout. But pushing through at all costs can have significant consequences for mental and physical health.

The World Health Organization defines burnout as "a syndrome conceptualized as resulting from chronic workplace stress that has not been successfully managed." Symptoms can include exhaustion, cynicism, and feelings of reduced professional efficacy. While grit can be a protective factor against stress by encouraging perseverance, excessive grit can lead to ignoring these warning signs. As you operate at your career peak, you are not immune to this. In fact, you have been at this journey for a long time. Maybe, you are now extra vulnerable to this. Do not ignore the signs.

A World-Class Athlete Shows Courage, Resilience Amid Mental Health Challenges

Simone Biles, widely regarded as one of the greatest gymnasts in history, not only captivates the world with her athletic prowess but also with her candidness about mental health. Her journey underscores the profound impact of psychological well-being on performance and serves as an inspirational example of resilience and self-awareness.

During the 2021 Tokyo Olympics, Biles faced an unexpected challenge known as the *twisties*, a condition that causes gymnasts to lose spatial awareness during routines, and poses significant safety risks. Recognizing the danger, she made the courageous decision to withdraw from multiple events to prioritize her mental health. She explains all about this in the documentary *Rising*.

While the twisties are a physical and neurological problem, apparently, they often stem from mental stress, anxiety, and psychological overload. Some in the public were critical of her decision to withdraw. In a *Vox* article Alex Abad-Santos, wrote, "What the public didn't fully understand and what Biles speaks about honestly in *Rising*, is that she believes the twisties she suffered in Tokyo were a result of unresolved stress and trauma." The article goes on to state, "Because of Covid-19 and the health precautions surrounding the pandemic, families were not allowed to travel with athletes to the 2021 Olympics. Biles's support system—her family and mom especially—was not present." In our formula, we would say a key part of her social capital was absent. Even at the peak, you don't make it alone.

In the aftermath, Biles openly discussed her therapeutic journey, and is quoted as saying, "In the beginning, I think the hardest part is logging on to my therapy sessions and convincing myself to go." However, she found solace in the process, noting that, "As soon as I see my therapist and we start talking, it's like I'm yapping the whole time. I'm so grateful for that."

In the 2024 Paris Olympics, Biles made a triumphant return and secured multiple medals that demonstrated her enduring excellence. Reflecting on the journey, she expressed no regrets about prioritizing her well-being, and reinforced the message that self-care is integral to sustained success.

Her openness about her mental health challenges and determination to address them head-on have not only solidified her legacy in gymnastics but have also paved the way for a broader acceptance of mental health prioritization in all walks of life.

To prevent burnout, it's crucial to recognize that rest, reflection, and personal well-being are not indulgences but necessities for long-term success. Building a sustainable approach to grit means knowing when to pause, recharge, and listen to the body's signals. In the end, resilience is about finding balance, not pushing through at the expense of health.

The Role of Mindfulness in Balancing Grit

Mindfulness—the practice of being fully present in the moment—can play a vital role in balancing grit and well-being. Research shows that mindfulness can reduce stress, improve focus, and even increase emotional resilience. Mindfulness can help high achievers reconnect with themselves, gain perspective on their goals, and prevent burnout by cultivating a more grounded approach to success.

One famous example of a leader who incorporates mindfulness into his routine is Marc Benioff, the CEO of Salesforce, a cloud-based software company. Haley Tenore wrote about him in *Business Insider*. It's clear Benioff credits mindfulness practices, including meditation and self-reflection, for helping him stay balanced amidst the demands of running a major corporation. Under his leadership, Salesforce has even incorporated mindfulness spaces into its corporate culture and encourages employees to take time for mental clarity.

Mindfulness doesn't require hours of meditation or a major lifestyle shift; it can be as simple as a pause to take a few deep breaths, the practice of gratitude, or even a few moments spent each day to reflect on personal goals. These practices help leaders and professionals maintain awareness of their needs, both physical and mental, and enable them to approach challenges with clarity rather than reacting impulsively.

To incorporate mindfulness into your life, start with small, manageable practices. Set aside five minutes each day for mindful breathing, journaling, or a quiet moment to reflect. Over time, these practices help build resilience, prevent burnout, and support a sustainable approach to grit.

Building Resilience through Self-Compassion

Self-compassion, the practice of treating oneself with kindness and understanding in times of failure or stress, can be an essential component of balanced grit. For many high achievers, self-criticism is a default response to setbacks, but research suggests that self-compassion is far more effective in promoting resilience. When we approach our own mistakes and challenges with empathy, we build a foundation for continued growth rather than eroding our self-esteem.

Psychologist Kristin Neff, a leading researcher on self-compassion, explains that self-compassion helps people stay resilient by providing emotional support in difficult times. People with high self-compassion are more likely to recover from failure, take responsibility for mistakes, and continue to pursue their goals without feeling overwhelmed by guilt or shame. In other words, self-compassion allows individuals to maintain grit without falling into self-destructive patterns.

To build self-compassion, practice treating yourself with the same kindness you would offer a friend. When you encounter setbacks, remind yourself that mistakes are part of the learning process. Reflect on what you can learn from each experience and celebrate your progress, rather than focusing on perfection. This approach nurtures a resilient mindset and supports a balanced form of grit that respects both ambition and well-being.

The Importance of Physical Health in Building Resilience

While mental resilience is crucial, physical health is an equally important aspect of balanced grit. Physical health directly impacts mental clarity, energy levels, and overall resilience. Regular exercise, proper nutrition, and sufficient sleep form the foundation of a healthy body, which, in turn, supports a resilient mind.

Ultra-marathoner Scott Jurek attributes his endurance to mental grit and also his commitment to physical health. Jurek has run some of the world's most grueling races, often covering distances of more than 100 miles in extreme conditions. By prioritizing nutrition, training, and recovery, Jurek sustains a career in one of the world's most demanding sports.

For professionals, maintaining physical health is equally vital. Leaders and high achievers who neglect their health in favor of work often find themselves facing fatigue, decreased productivity, and an increased risk of burnout. Exercise, even in small amounts, can improve mood, boost energy, and enhance focus. Prioritizing physical health is an investment in long-term resilience.

To build resilience through physical health, start by setting realistic goals. Commit to a balanced diet, incorporate physical activity into your routine, and prioritize sleep. These habits enhance your physical health as well as support mental well-being, and that enables you to maintain grit without sacrificing vitality.

Boundaries: Know When to Say No

One of the most challenging aspects of balanced grit is learning to set boundaries. High achievers often feel compelled to say "yes" to every opportunity, fearing that turning something down might mean missing out. But overcommitment can lead to burnout, making it essential to recognize when to say "no" in order to protect one's well-being.

Steve Jobs was known for his intense focus and willingness to say "no" to ideas that didn't align with Apple's core vision. He believed that innovation required discipline, and part of that discipline was to protect his time and energy for the projects that mattered most. His ability to set boundaries allowed him to maintain clarity, prioritize effectively, and drive Apple's success.

For professionals, setting boundaries means understanding your limits and protecting your time for the most important tasks. Evaluate opportunities carefully and be mindful of how each commitment aligns with your goals. Learn to say "no" when necessary, and you will preserve energy for the pursuits that truly matter, creating a sustainable path to success.

Sustain Grit with a Balanced Approach to Success

Grit is essential to achieve long-term success; but without balance, it can lead to burnout and diminish well-being. By incorporating mindfulness, self-compassion, physical health, and social support, you build a foundation that allows you to sustain resilience without compromising health. Balance isn't about sacrificing ambition; it's about creating a sustainable path to growth, one that respects both the drive for success and the need for rest.

Leaders and professionals who balance grit with well-being don't just achieve success; they achieve it in a way that's fulfilling, sustainable, and inspiring to others. By embracing this balanced approach, you can maintain the resilience to face challenges, the energy to pursue goals, and the clarity to lead a meaningful life. This harmony between grit and well-being enables you to sustain success over the long term, leaving a legacy of resilience, compassion, and balanced ambition. Remember – "you ARE NOT invincible."

13

Peak-Career Exercise

Hone Your Final Approach and Envision Your Future

It's time to say goodbye, but I think goodbyes are sad, and I'd much rather say hello. Hello to a new adventure.
—Ernie Harwell

Objective: This exercise helps peak-career professionals take stock of where they are, assess how their strengths fit with evolving opportunities, and chart a deliberate course toward a more fulfilling next chapter.

To Get Started: Set aside uninterrupted time to work through the prompts and frameworks that follow. These exercises encourage honest reflection on what energizes you and where you create the most value. Each section is timed to help you focus without overthinking. There are no right or wrong answers—only insights to guide your journey.

Peak-Career Playbook: A Six-Step Strategy for Legacy, Influence, and Renewal Designed for Peak-Career Professionals (Likely Ages 51+)

Each module incorporates deep reflection, strategic engagement, and structured outputs to help you solidify your impact—and shape what comes next.

STEP 1: *Legacy Reflection and Impact Inventory*

Duration: 45 minutes
Purpose: Take stock of your professional footprint and begin to define your legacy.

Prompted Deep Dive

Answer in a dedicated journal or digital doc:

- What accomplishments am I most proud of in my career?
- How has my work shaped people, teams, or institutions?
- What do I want to be remembered for?
- Are there areas where I still feel unfulfilled?

Career Thesis Format

Draft a single sentence that starts with:

- "How have I created value . . ."
- "My work matters because . . ."
- "Over this peak phase, I will contribute to the world by . . ."

Peer Debrief (Optional but Powerful)

Collaborate with a colleague for a 20-minute session:

- Share the points in your thesis and have them challenge it with "Why?" "So what?" and "For whom?"
- Refine your statements based on the conversation

Visualization Exercise Imagine your retirement celebration. What are others saying about your legacy? What stories are told about your influence and impact?

STEP 2: Optimize Your Current Role

Duration: 1 hour
Purpose: Maximize the impact of your current position and invest in the next generation.

Actions to Consider

- Identify key systems, teams, or programs where your wisdom can drive improvement.
- Launch a mentoring initiative or formalize your coaching of emerging leaders.
- Speak at internal events or town halls to share strategic insight.
- Champion efforts aligned with your values—mentorship, culture, innovation, or service.

STEP 3: Extend Your Reach Beyond Your Role

Duration: 90 minutes
Purpose: Contribute your expertise in broader, more flexible ways.

Engagement Pathways

- Join a nonprofit board, industry council, or school advisory group.
- Deliver guest lectures or workshops in your area of expertise.
- Publish articles or op-eds that reflect your leadership perspective.
- Explore pro bono or consulting work that aligns with your personal mission.

STEP 4: Align Life and Work for the Next Chapter

Duration: 1 hour
Purpose: Reflect on how your time and energy align with what matters most—and plan forward.

Prompted Life Audit

- How do I currently spend my time—and how do I want to spend it?
- What gives me the most energy now (and what drains it)?
- What does "success" look like over the next 10–15 years?
- What are my family, health, and lifestyle considerations?

- When I leave my current vocation and enter my "second life," what would I not want to change, and what would I like to do differently? Make a simple list for now.

Scenario Planning Explore phased retirement, creative projects, part-time board service, or full reinvention.

STEP 5: *Quarterly Legacy Calibration*

Duration: 30 minutes (every 90 days)
Purpose: Stay focused on your values, impact, and evolving sense of purpose.

Legacy Journal Prompts

- What did I help others achieve this quarter?
- What legacy-building effort did I advance?
- What changed in me—and how should that affect my roadmap?

Optional Peer Reflection Ask two to three trusted colleagues:

- "Where am I creating the most value right now?"
- "What would you miss most if I left?"

STEP 6: *Celebrate and Share Your Journey*

Duration: 30 minutes
Purpose: Cement your contributions, express gratitude, and inspire others.

Ways to Share

- Create a "Legacy Portfolio" of projects, people, and principles you've influenced.
- Host a conversation or fireside chat reflecting on key lessons.
- Publish a short essay or blog on "What I've Learned."
- Shine a light on your mentors and mentees—legacy is shared, not solo.

Final Output: Legacy Strategy Canvas

At the end of this playbook, you should have:

- A clearly articulated Legacy Vision
- A Personal Impact Portfolio
- A Mentorship and Influence Plan
- A Vision for Transition or Reinvention
- A Legacy Dashboard (updated quarterly)

PART IV

Post-Career: Coming Down the Mountain After the Peak

14 | Deciding If, When, and How to Retire

> You know you're doing what you love when Sunday night feels the same as Friday night... but when it doesn't, maybe it's time to reconsider.
>
> —Warren Buffett

The potential dilemma executives face later in their careers is if, when, and how to retire. I can't count how often I get calls from retired executives who say, "You have to find me a job. Retirement is not for me." Some of these calls are from former top executives who are now unfulfilled, even while serving on multiple corporate boards, playing a lot of golf, and traveling to exotic places. They tell me they are tired of giving advice. They actually want to lead and make things happen.

My conclusion from the conversations is that for many people—even perhaps most people—the career journey to the peak was the fun part. After that peak, they can get lost, or at least bored and lonely.

If you have the option of extending your current career journey, you are fortunate and may decide to continue as is. I believe that when it's time to leave your current career path, you will somehow intuitively know it. It can be a deeply emotional time. Some simply hit the wall and know it's time for a change. If this is not yet clear to you, I suggest you continue on knowing that retirement is always an option when the time is right.

You've Decided to Make the Change—Now What?

Once you decide to make the change, there's lots to consider. The summit of a career, much like the peak of a mountain, offers a spectacular view. It is a moment of pride and reflection, a testament to decades of effort, sacrifice, and resilience.

Yet for many professionals, a curious realization emerges at this stage: "Getting here was a lot more fun than being here." The thrill of the climb, with its challenges and rewards, is often replaced by a plateau where the excitement of upward momentum fades. This moment invites an important question, what's next?

We are living longer, healthier lives. The traditional trajectory of a career might span 35–45 years. Then you may have another 25 years—or more—of vibrant, capable life ahead. This is not a time for retreat but a time to renew, explore new paths, and find fresh meaning in both professional and personal endeavors. Coming down the mountain is not about decline; it is about recalibrating and continuing to ascend, albeit in new directions.

The "Second Life"

Davide Casolino coined this label, "second life" for me.

Casolino's professional journey reflects a remarkable blend of technical brilliance, visionary partnership, and meaningful contribution to medical innovation. Graduating from a leading university in Milan in the early 1980s with a degree in software engineering, Casolino entered the professional world during a time when computing power was just beginning to find its place in specialized fields, such as healthcare. His early academic foundation in algorithmic design, systems architecture, and computer graphics laid the groundwork for a revolutionary career at the intersection of technology and medicine.

Davide's path took a decisive turn when he partnered with Cesare Giorgi, a distinguished neurosurgeon with deep expertise in the treatment of brain tumors. Together, they recognized a crucial need in oncology: the ability to improve the precision and planning of radiological interventions for brain tumors. Traditional radiotherapy techniques at the time were limited in their ability to target tumors accurately without damaging surrounding healthy tissue—particularly critical in the brain, where millimeter-level precision can mean the difference between preserving or impairing essential functions.

In 1991, Davide Casolino, Enrico Ongania, Marco Luzzara, and Professor Cesere Giorgi co-founded 3D Line Medical Systems S.r.l. in Milan. Casolino led the company's technical strategy, developing sophisticated software platforms that transformed the planning and delivery of radiation therapy. In the mid-nineties, 3D Line created systems that enabled high-precision stereotactic radiosurgery (SRS) and intensity-modulated radiation therapy (IMRT), two cutting-edge approaches designed to deliver focused, high-dose radiation to tumors while minimizing exposure to healthy brain tissue. Starting this business took the 5Qs for sure. They were going up against multinational giants who were already entrenched in the medical imaging industry. No pun intended; this was a David-versus-Goliath scenario.

One of their flagship products was ERGO++, a powerful treatment planning system that allowed oncologists to visualize tumors in three dimensions, calculate optimal radiation paths, and simulate treatment outcomes. The platform used advanced algorithms to model patient anatomy and radiation beam behavior with unprecedented accuracy, drastically improving the predictability and effectiveness of brain tumor treatments. Casolino's background in software engineering was critical in translating complex medical requirements into intuitive, high-performance applications that clinicians could use reliably.

In addition to ERGO++, 3D Line developed DYNART™, a micro-multileaf collimator system that physically shaped radiation beams during therapy, enhancing treatment flexibility and allowing practitioners to better conform the radiation dose to the intricate contours of brain tumors.

The company's technologies quickly attracted attention from the international medical community for their innovation and clinical impact. By the mid-2000s, 3D Line had become a recognized leader in precision radiotherapy solutions, particularly for neurosurgical applications. In 2007, the Swedish company Elekta AB, a global leader in oncology and neuroscience treatment systems, acquired 3D Line. The acquisition was strategic: Elekta sought to integrate 3D Line's planning and beam-shaping innovations into its broader portfolio, advancing its capabilities in treating brain and spinal tumors.

Through this acquisition, Casolino's technical vision reached a global scale, influencing the way radiation oncology is practiced around the world. His journey—from a Milanese university lecture hall to the forefront of medical technology innovation—stands as a testament to the power of interdisciplinary collaboration, persistent technical advancement, and a commitment to improving patient outcomes. Passion drove Casolino and his partners.

I was fortunate to meet Davide after he had started what he calls his *second life*. I had a couple days off between meetings in Europe in April 2025. So, I found a company that provided fishing guides in the Lake Como region. They connected me with a guy named Davide to go pike fishing. He had a small skiff, with a small outboard tiller motor. He was dressed in a tee-shirt and a pair of work shorts. He looked like a 60-year-old who worked as a laborer turned fisherman—nothing fancy about him. How was I supposed to know he was a famous software engineer?

After about an hour on the boat, I asked him if this was his primary job. He looked at me and said, "Actually, this is my second life." That's when I learned the person who was helping me put bait on my fishing line and operate the little 16-foot fishing boat, was actually a brilliant, retired software engineer whose business had sold for millions of dollars. Davide embodies much of what we are teaching in the book about ways to move on to your next phase after you have reached your initial Greatness Objective. His story will help you think about possibilities for your own life.

Davide asked me to share this: "Regarding my second life, I would like to point out that I have adopted the same principle as when I operated in the global market. I hope you have noticed that going fishing with me does not only mean 'fishing', but a unique experience where we talk about technology, effects of climate change, perfect knowledge of the environment, all united by the desire to transmit this passion to my guests." Perfectly said—will you do something in your next phase that ties in with all you learned in your first phase? The good news is *you* get to choose. Go for it!

What Might You Do in Your Second Life?

Those phone calls I receive from retirees demonstrate that for some, full retirement can be a disappointment, so extending a professional career by assembling a portfolio of work is an option to explore. This might mean a shift from full-time roles to consulting, mentoring, or part-time positions that allow for continued engagement without the demands of a traditional job. For others, it might mean taking on advisory or board roles where experience and wisdom are valued. For others still, it may be a fishing boat, bed and breakfast, or who-knows-what-else.

If you worked in the trades in your own business, you may choose to cut back by working for a company in your trade instead. That cuts the stress of running your own business, but keeps you busy and fulfilled as you continue to ply your trade.

I have friends who worked in the trades and, after years of work, didn't feel they could continue to endure the physical pressure of their jobs. In that case, they may want to consider working for a retailer who sells supplies related to their trade, or another option could be to get a certification to teach apprentice programs for those entering their trade.

Regardless of whether your career was corporate, teaching, in the trades, or some other vocation, there is a way to assemble a portfolio to stay engaged.

Many find that stepping away from their original profession enables the pursuit of passions relegated to the margins during their primary career. Teaching, writing, or exploring entrepreneurship are all pathways that can transform years of expertise into something innovative and rewarding. For example, one might mentor young entrepreneurs, write a memoir to share their journey, or start a small business rooted in a lifelong hobby.

Here are more suggestions:

- **Start a small business:** Consider turning a passion or niche expertise into a small business. Whether it's a consulting practice, an e-commerce store, or a boutique service. Platforms like SCORE (Senior Corps of Retired Executives, a nonprofit) or local Small Business Administration (SBA) offices can provide resources to get started.

- **Executive coaching:** Help the next generation of leaders thrive by becoming an executive coach. Programs such as the International Coaching Federation (ICF) certification can provide training and credentials.
- **Teach or write:** Explore adjunct teaching roles at universities or community colleges, or contribute to industry publications. These activities help share your expertise and keep you intellectually engaged.
- **Advisory roles with private equity or venture capital firms:** These firms often seek seasoned professionals to guide portfolio companies or evaluate investment opportunities. Leverage your industry network and attend venture capital or private equity conferences, or join groups like the National Association of Corporate Directors (NACD). Networking on platforms like LinkedIn or through professional organizations can also open doors.
- **Serve on boards:** Explore roles on public or private company boards, which value the strategic insights and governance experience of seasoned executives.

Retirement Planning: A Step-by-Step Process

Retirement is one of the most significant decisions a person will face in their lifetime. Unlike career transitions or promotions, retirement represents the culmination of decades of effort and the start of a new phase of life. It's a deeply personal decision, influenced by financial readiness, emotional preparedness, health considerations, and personal goals.

To make this decision thoughtfully, it's essential to evaluate multiple factors, anticipate challenges, and create a plan for post-retirement life. This chapter outlines a detailed, step-by-step process to help individuals determine when and if they should retire.

Assess Your Financial Readiness

Financial security is one of the most critical components of a successful retirement. Without a solid financial foundation, retirement can quickly become a source of stress rather than relaxation and fulfillment. Here are a few steps that can help someone evaluate their financial readiness. First, understand your retirement expenses:

- Create a comprehensive budget that accounts for essential expenses (housing, utilities, food), discretionary spending (travel, hobbies), and potential healthcare costs.
- Factor in inflation and unexpected expenses.

Calculate your retirement income:

- Assess all sources of retirement income, including:
    - Social Security benefits
    - Pension plans
    - Retirement savings accounts like 401(k)s and IRAs
    - Investment income, including stock dividends and rental properties
    - Annuities or other guaranteed income sources
- Use online tools or work with a financial advisor to project how long your savings will last.

Next, determine your withdrawal strategy, including:

- Follow the 4 percent rule or other withdrawal strategies to ensure your savings last throughout retirement. ChatGPT, using natural language processing can tell you how long your savings will last by simply crafting the right prompt with your current financial data.
- Adjust your strategy for longevity, market fluctuations, and personal spending habits.

Evaluate debt and liabilities:

- Pay down high-interest debt, such as credit cards or personal loans, before retiring.
- Consider refinancing or paying off a mortgage if it aligns with your financial goals.

Engage a financial planner to help:

- A certified financial planner (CFP) can provide objective advice and help you model different retirement scenarios.
- Discuss tax implications of withdrawing from retirement accounts and strategies for minimizing taxes.

Consider Your Emotional Preparedness

While financial readiness is critical, emotional preparedness often determines whether retirement feels like an exciting new chapter or a disorienting loss of purpose. Honestly evaluate your future so you are less likely to be one of those people who are compelled to call people like me to look for a job after they first chose to *retire*.

Some questions to ask yourself include:

1. What does retirement mean to you?
   - Do you view retirement as freedom from work or an opportunity to pursue new passions?
   - Are you excited about the prospect of more free time, or does the thought of leaving work behind make you uneasy?
2. How will you spend your time?
   - Develop a vision for your days in retirement. Consider activities like travel, volunteering, spending time with family, or pursuing hobbies.
   - Avoid the *retirement void* where a lack of purpose leads to dissatisfaction.
3. Do you have a support system?
   - Retirement often changes social dynamics. Consider how you will maintain connections and engage with your community.
   - Discuss your plans with family and close friends to ensure alignment and understanding.
4. Are you ready to let go of your professional identity?
   - Many professionals derive a sense of self-worth from their careers. Reflect on how you will transition to a new identity and purpose.

Actionable Steps for Emotional Preparedness

- **Transition gradually:** Consider a reduction in your hours or shift to a consulting or advisory role before fully retiring.
- **Engage in pre-retirement counseling:** Some organizations offer programs to help employees plan for the emotional aspects of retirement.
- **Create a retirement trial run:** Take an extended vacation or sabbatical to experience life without the structure of work.

Evaluate Your Health and Longevity

Health plays a significant role in retirement timing. While you can't predict every aspect of your health, you can make informed decisions based on your current condition and family history.

Some factors to consider include:

1. Current health status and future considerations:
   - Assess any chronic conditions or physical limitations that could impact your ability to work or enjoy retirement.
   - Schedule a comprehensive health check-up to understand your medical needs.
2. Family health history:
   - Consider longevity trends in your family. If your relatives tend to live long, healthy lives, you may plan for a longer retirement phase.
3. Healthcare costs:
   - Plan for medical expenses, including insurance premiums, deductibles, and out-of-pocket costs.
   - Explore long-term care insurance or savings strategies to cover future needs.
4. The impact of work on your health:
   - Reflect on how your career affects your physical and mental health. If work-related stress is harming your well-being, retiring earlier may be a better option.

Actionable Steps for Health Evaluation

- **Consult healthcare professionals:** Work with your doctor to create a long-term health plan.
- **Stay active:** Develop an exercise routine and focus on a healthy lifestyle, regardless of whether you continue working.
- **Review Medicare and insurance options:** Understand when you're eligible for Medicare and how it fits into your retirement health plan.

Align Retirement Timing with Personal Goals

Retirement is not just about leaving the workforce; it's about transitioning into a phase that aligns with your life goals.

Clarify your life priorities. That includes answering the following questions:

1. What do you want to accomplish post-retirement?
   - Make a list of goals like traveling, learning new skills, spending time with loved ones, or giving back to the community.
2. What milestones are important to you?
   - Consider timing retirement around significant personal events like a child's graduation, move to a new home, or achievement of a specific savings goal.
3. What legacy do you want to leave?
   - Reflect on how you can use retirement to contribute to causes you care about or pass on knowledge and values to future generations.

Explore Flexible Retirement Options

Retirement doesn't have to be an all-or-nothing decision. Many professionals find fulfillment in semi-retirement or phased retirement arrangements. A few popular flexible retirement models include:

- **Part-time work:** Transition to a part-time schedule in your current field.
    Consulting or freelancing: Use your expertise to work on specific projects or advise organizations.

- **Advisory or board roles:** Serve as a board member or advisor for companies or nonprofits.
- **Entrepreneurship:** Start a small business based on your interests or hobbies.

Benefits of a flexible retirement include maintaining ongoing income, keeping yourself mentally and socially engaged, and offering a smoother transition into full retirement.

Anticipate Challenges and Plan for Solutions

Retirement is a significant life change and may bring unexpected challenges. By anticipating these hurdles, you can create strategies to navigate them successfully.

Common Challenges

1. **Loss of structure:** Without the routine of work, some retirees feel aimless or unproductive.
   - Solution: Establish a daily schedule with planned activities.
2. **Financial anxiety:** Even with careful planning, retirees may worry about running out of money.
   - Solution: Revisit your financial plan annually and adjust spending if needed.
3. **Social isolation:** Leaving the workplace may result in fewer social interactions.
   - Solution: Join clubs, volunteer, or take classes to build new relationships.
4. **Marital adjustments:** Retirement can shift dynamics in relationships, especially if one partner retires while the other continues working.
   - Solution: Communicate openly with your partner about expectations and boundaries.

Create a Comprehensive Written Retirement Plan

After considering all this, it's time to write things down. A written retirement plan serves as a roadmap for this life transition. It helps clarify your goals and provides a framework for decision-making.

Components of that retirement plan include what we have previously noted:

1. Financial plan
   - Monthly budget and income projections.
   - Investment strategy and withdrawal schedule.
2. Healthcare plan
   - Insurance coverage and anticipated medical costs.
3. Lifestyle plan
   - Daily activities, engaging in new work, hobbies, travel, and personal development goals.
4. Legacy plan
   - Estate planning, charitable contributions, and family priorities.

Professionals can provide valuable guidance to ensure your retirement plan is well-rounded and realistic. Some of those professionals can include:

- **Financial advisors:** Help evaluate your financial readiness and create a sustainable plan.
- **Retirement coaches:** Assist with the emotional and psychological aspects of retirement.
- **Healthcare consultants:** Guide you through Medicare, insurance options, and long-term care planning.
- **Estate planners:** Ensure your assets are distributed according to your wishes.

Transitioning from your career at retirement age isn't an end—it's the beginning of your *second life*. With thoughtful planning and a sense of purpose, this next chapter can be deeply rewarding, offering new opportunities for growth, contribution, and fulfillment beyond the traditional boundaries of work. Korn Ferry helps companies seeking to assist their employees through this transition.

15

Public Company Board Service

A Step-by-Step Guide

Pathway to Public Company Board Service

I served on the board of a multi-billion dollar company for more than a decade. I have placed dozens of executives on boards. For many retired or semi-retired professionals, serving on a public company board offers a compelling way to stay intellectually engaged, contribute at the highest levels of strategy, and leverage decades of leadership insight. Yet earning a seat at the boardroom table requires far more than a stellar résumé. It demands a deliberate, disciplined approach to positioning, visibility, and network cultivation. I get calls weekly from people who would like to join a public company board. I have worked with clients to place dozens of executives onto public boards. It is a very fragmented market. Many qualified people fail to attain board membership. However, with diligence and a strong outreach campaign, it can be done. I suggest that the outreach take the form of an email campaign. You should use your social capital network to contact as many as 100 people in your network who serve on boards. Let them know you are now available. Solicit their advice. Don't ask them if you can join a board they are involved with. They will certainly keep you in mind without you imposing on them directly. Often, they will hear about board openings from their own networks, and because of your outreach, they will likely suggest you as someone worthy of consideration. Then, you may get a call. Below is a refined roadmap to help you navigate the journey.

Step 1: Assess Your Board Readiness

- C-suite or equivalent P&L leadership—especially CEO, CFO, or divisional head roles.
- Functional expertise in areas such as finance, audit, digital transformation, cybersecurity, M&A, compliance, or ESG.
- Governance familiarity through service on public, private, nonprofit, or advisory boards.
- **Recommended resource:** "The Handbook of Board Governance" by Richard Leblanc.

Step 2: Develop a Compelling Board Bio and Résumé

- **Board biography:** A succinct one-page narrative emphasizing your governance lens, leadership journey, and what you uniquely contribute at the board level.
- **Board résumé:** Tailored to highlight strategic decision-making, enterprise risk management, capital allocation, digital initiatives, and organizational transformation.
- **Recommended resource:** BoardProspects.com résumé builder and the National Association of Corporate Directors (NACD) templates.

Step 3: Build a Board-Level Personal Brand

- Publish thought leadership in outlets like Harvard Business Review, Directors & Boards, or Agenda Week.
- Speak at governance events hosted by The Conference Board, NACD, or industry associations.
- Optimize your LinkedIn profile to emphasize board competencies and interests.
- **Recommended resources:** "Get on Board" by Nancy Falls; LinkedIn's "Board Aspirations" groups.

Step 4: Expand Your Strategic Network

- Engage directly with sitting directors at events or alumni networks.
- Join professional organizations such as NACD, PDA, WCD, Ascend Pinnacle.
- Introduce yourself to search firms: Egon Zehnder, Heidrick & Struggles, Spencer Stuart.
- Refer back to the I-CARD methodology to expand your network each year.

Step 5: Gain Practical Governance Experience

- Join nonprofit or foundation boards to learn about fiduciary responsibility.
- Serve on private company advisory boards.
- Participate in internal governance councils.
- **Recommended resource:** BoardStrong.org for nonprofit board matching.

Step 6: Pursue Formal Board Education and Certification

- NACD Directorship Certification.
- Stanford Directors' College.
- Harvard Business School's Board Programs.
- University of Chicago Booth's Director's Consortium.
- **Recommended resource:** Corporate Governance Training from the NACD, or Harvard or Wharton.

Step 7: Target Companies Where You Add Unique Value

- Mid-cap or recently IPO'd companies where your functional or industry expertise is critical.
- Companies undergoing transformation or scaling globally.
- Analyze proxy statements (DEF 14A) to understand current board needs.
- **Recommended tools:** BoardEx; Equilar BoardEdge.

Step 8: Master the Board Interview Process
- Demonstrate fluency in industry and governance trends.
- Balance collegiality with independence.
- Communicate your board value proposition.
- **Recommended resource:** See Dan Byrne's guide published by *The Corporate Governance Institute*.

Step 9: Stay Engaged and Continue Learning
- Attend director forums like NACD Summit.
- Subscribe to governance publications like *Harvard Law School Forum, Corporate Board Member, Boardroom Insider*.
- Seek informal mentorship from board leaders.

A board seat is both a capstone and a continuation—a distinguished opportunity to serve, shape, and safeguard value for future generations. The path requires intentional positioning, strategic visibility, and governance fluency—but for those ready, it offers purpose, impact, and deep professional satisfaction.

16

Engage with Private Equity and Venture Capital

A Post-Career Opportunity

Let's explore the private equity (PE) and venture capital (VC) markets in more detail. I am often asked for advice on how to access this community to potentially get one last executive role, to serve as a board member in a portfolio company, or to serve as an operating partner. I am a limited partner in both a VC and a PE fund. A great way to set yourself up for future roles with private equity and venture capital is to become an investor while you are still working during mid or peak career phases. Then, when you look to move into a portfolio career with venture or private equity as a component, you are already a known entity to the general partners and even the portfolio companies. I strongly suggest this approach.

PE and VC firms present exciting opportunities for retired executives to leverage their expertise, build on their careers, and engage in impactful advisory roles. These firms often seek experienced professionals to guide portfolio companies, assist with deal evaluations, or serve as operating partners.

Below is a step-by-step guide to identify and approach these firms and understand the opportunities they offer.

Step 1: Understand Private Equity and Venture Capital Advisory Roles

Advisors in PE and VC firms typically perform one or more of the following functions:

- **Operating partners:** Work closely with portfolio companies to improve operations, streamline processes, and accelerate growth.
- **Advisory board members:** Work with deal partners or with individual portfolio companies without serving directly on a governance board.
- **Board members:** Serve on the boards of portfolio companies, providing strategic oversight and governance.
- **Sector experts:** Offer insights into specific industries to guide investment decisions.
- **Due diligence advisors:** Evaluate potential acquisitions or investments, focusing on risks, market dynamics, and operational efficiencies.

Why Firms Seek Retired Executives   Retired executives bring valuable skills that include:

- Deep industry expertise and operational experience.
- Established networks for business development, talent acquisition, and partnerships.
- Proven leadership in navigating challenges such as turnarounds, scaling, or regulatory compliance.

Step 2: Research and Identify Target PE and VC Firms

Categorize Firms by Focus

Private equity and venture capital firms vary widely in their investment strategies and industries. It's critical to identify firms aligned with your expertise.

- Private equity firms:
    - **Focus:** mature companies with potential for operational improvement or financial restructuring.
    - **Typical targets:** mid-market to large companies across sectors like healthcare, manufacturing, consumer goods, and technology.
    - **Examples:** Blackstone, KKR, TPG, FTV, Carlyle Group, Bain Capital.
- Venture Capital Firms:
    - **Focus:** early-stage or growth-stage startups.
    - **Typical targets:** technology, healthcare, fintech, and clean energy companies.
    - **Examples:** Sequoia Capital, Andreessen Horowitz, NYCA, Benchmark Capital.
- Sector-specific firms:
    - Some firms specialize in niches like life sciences, renewable energy, or logistics.
    - Use tools like PitchBook or Crunchbase to identify firms with a sector focus that matches your expertise.

Research Firms and Their Portfolios

- Use PitchBook, CB Insights, Preqin, or Crunchbase to research firm profiles, portfolio companies, and leadership teams.
- Visit firm websites to understand their investment focus and recent deals.
- Review annual reports and industry publications for insights into firm strategies and performance.

Look for Regional Connections
- Identify firms with investments or offices in your geographic area for easier networking.

Step 3: Build a Personal Brand Aligned with PE and VC Needs

Craft a Strong Value Proposition

Articulate how your expertise can directly benefit PE and VC firms. Highlight:

- Leadership roles where you drove growth, efficiency, or innovation.
- Specific accomplishments, such as successful mergers, product launches, or market expansions.
- Strategic initiatives where you improved company performance.

Prepare a Compelling Profile
- **Board-style résumé:** Emphasize governance, strategic oversight, and operational success.
- **LinkedIn profile:**
  - Optimize your headline to include keywords like "advisor," "board member," or "industry expert."
  - Showcase specific achievements that align with investment firm priorities.

Engage in Thought Leadership
- Write articles, blogs, or white papers on trends in your industry or operational best practices.
- Speak at industry conferences or webinars to establish your expertise.

Step 4: Leverage Your Network

Activate Existing Relationships
- Reach out to colleagues, mentors, and professional contacts with connections to private equity or venture capital firms.
- Share your interest in advisory roles and ask for introductions.

Attend Industry Events

Attending events and joining various forums are helpful, but direct outreach is most effective. Some ways to do that include:

- Conferences like Informa Connect's SuperReturn Events (for PE) and TechCrunch Disrupt (for VC) among many others are excellent networking opportunities.
- Utilize professional networks like World 50, ExecThread, or BoardProspects to broaden your network and connect with PE and VC professionals.
- Engage with alumni groups or executive associations that often have connections to investment firms.

Step 5: Approach Firms Strategically

Identify the Right Contact
- Research the leadership team on the firm's website or LinkedIn.
- Reach out to managing partners, principals, or operating partners who oversee portfolio operations.
- Use your social capital network for an introduction whenever possible.

Tailor Your Outreach
- Initial email or LinkedIn message
  - Be concise and specific.
  - Highlight your relevant experience and express your interest in contributing as an advisor.
  - Sample

> "Dear [Name], I'm impressed with [Firm's Name]'s work in transforming companies in [sector]. With more than 25 years of experience leading operational turnarounds and scaling businesses in this industry, I'd be excited to contribute as an advisor to your portfolio companies. Having reviewed your list of portfolio companies, I believe I can make potential customer introductions and offer product advancement suggestions. I'd welcome the opportunity to discuss how my expertise might align with your objectives."

- Follow-up meeting
  - Prepare to discuss how you can address specific challenges or opportunities for their portfolio companies.
  - Share examples of past successes, emphasizing results.

Step 6: Explore Entry Points into the Various Roles

Start with Short-Term Consulting
- Offer to work on a specific project, like evaluating an acquisition or developing a go-to-market strategy for a portfolio company.
- This allows the firm to assess your value and can lead to more permanent roles.

Seek an Operating Partner Role
- PE firms appoint executives to more formalized roles often called operating partners.
- Typically, it calls for a deeper time commitment from the executive and a more formal compensation scheme from the firm.

Join Advisory Boards
- Many PE and VC firms create advisory boards composed of industry experts who provide strategic guidance across the portfolio.

Offer Mentorship
- VC firms often seek experienced executives to mentor startup founders. This can lead to deeper involvement as the startup grows.

Step 7: Demonstrate Value During Engagements

Key Contributions Firms Expect
- **Operational expertise:** Help portfolio companies improve margins, reduce costs, or streamline operations.
- **Strategic oversight:** Provide guidance on market positioning, product development, or competitive strategy.

- **Access to networks:** Leverage your relationships to connect firms with potential customers, partners, or talent.
- **Governance:** Serve on the board of portfolio companies to ensure adherence to strategic goals and compliance.

Example: Operating Partner at a PE Firm

A retired COO with a history of turning around underperforming divisions joins a PE firm as an operating partner. They work directly with portfolio companies, to identify inefficiencies and implement performance improvement plans.

Step 8: Expand and Deepen Relationships

Once you've established a relationship with a PE or VC firm, continue to expand your involvement.

How to Stay Engaged

- Regularly attend firm events like partner meetings or portfolio reviews.
- Pursue appointments to portfolio company boards.
- Volunteer for additional projects to showcase your versatility.
- Provide referrals for investment opportunities or talent acquisition.
- Meet with portfolio company executives.
- Meet with the head of talent for the firm.

Example: Board Member for a VC Portfolio Company

An experienced technology executive joins the board of a growth-stage SaaS (software as a service) company funded by a VC firm. They use their industry knowledge to refine the company's strategy with a successful acquisition as a result.

Step 9: Evaluate and Choose the Right Fit

Not every PE or VC firm will align with your goals or values. Be selective in choosing engagements that resonate with your expertise and interests.

Questions to Ask Before Committing

- Who are the general partners?
- What is the firm's investment philosophy and approach to working with advisors?
  - What is their track record measured by investment results and industry reputation?
  - Who are their limited partners?
  - How involved are advisors in day-to-day portfolio company operations?
  - What is the expected time commitment and compensation structure?

Final Thoughts on Private Markets During This Phase of Your Life

Involvement with private equity and venture capital firms offers retired executives a meaningful way to stay engaged, apply their expertise, and shape the success of companies. An executive can open doors to exciting new opportunities in this dynamic space by proactively identifying target firms, building a compelling personal brand, leveraging their networks, and demonstrating value in advisory roles.

With careful planning and persistence, this path can be a fulfilling next chapter following a successful career.

Postscript

A Note About the Importance of 5Q, Greatness Code, Organizational Culture

There are many companies with exceptional cultures that foster greatness. Not enough for my liking, but they do exist. As just two very different examples, I share a short history of Goldman Sachs and also the London Stock Exchange Group (LSEG), demonstrating that *organizations* can exhibit the 5Qs we study in this book. While every organization has issues and stumbles, there is plenty of bad press out there about almost any organization, and in some cases, they deserve to be criticized. I offer these examples with that caveat. They are not perfect, yet they do strive for perfection and set a positive example. They have achieved success in ways that overall reflect well on their leadership and cultures.

Goldman Sachs: A Legacy Built on the 5Qs of Greatness

For more than 150 years, Goldman Sachs has stood at the intersection of ambition, adversity, and achievement. From its modest beginnings in 1869 as a small commercial paper business founded by Marcus Goldman, the firm evolved through decades of economic upheaval, wars, depressions, and transformations in global finance. Its survival—and dominance—has not been the product of luck or timing alone. Rather, Goldman Sachs has been built, expanded, and redefined by individuals who embodied the five qualities at the core of *The Greatness Code*: persistence, resilience, courage, passion, and stamina.

Persistence

Persistence was evident from the start. Marcus Goldman arrived in America as a German immigrant with little more than an idea and a fierce work ethic. He persevered through uncertain financial climates, laying the groundwork for a firm that would thrive through some of the most volatile eras in global economics. Generations of leaders followed suit, persisting through regulatory upheaval, financial crises, and relentless competition.

Resilience

Resilience became Goldman's calling card during the Great Depression and again during the 2008 financial crisis. In both cases, the firm endured and emerged stronger—not simply by reacting, but by adapting its model, embracing new leadership, and rethinking its strategy in real time. Goldman's ability to rebound has always been anchored in deep institutional learning and leadership willing to reframe risk and reinvent roles.

Courage

Courage has fueled the firm's willingness to break conventions—from pioneering the IPO market in the early 1900s to taking itself public in 1999, after 130 years as a private partnership. It took courage to lead major restructurings of industries, to advise on contentious mergers, and to make bold bets on market trends before they were obvious to the rest of Wall Street.

Passion

Passion is perhaps Goldman's most underappreciated asset. Behind its sharp suits and disciplined demeanor is a culture driven by intellectual passion—a hunger to solve problems, innovate products, and serve clients with intensity. That passion has drawn some of the brightest minds in business, economics, and public service, all united by an appetite for excellence and continuous improvement.

Stamina

Stamina may be the trait that best explains Goldman's longevity. Markets may swing, reputations may cycle, but the firm's ability to withstand pressure over decades—while continuing to evolve—is a testament to sustained high performance at the individual and organizational level. Whether navigating regulatory scrutiny, internal restructuring, or global disruption, Goldman Sachs has shown it can play the long game.

While Goldman has not been a big client of mine, I have many friends who have worked there over the years. They were super smart, had high integrity, and were fiercely driven to achieve. The Goldman Sachs story isn't just about financial acumen—it's about the human qualities that power long-term greatness. The firm's leaders and culture have repeatedly demonstrated the 5Qs not as abstract ideals, but as daily disciplines. That's why Goldman Sachs doesn't just survive in a brutal industry—it shapes it.

London Stock Exchange Group (LSEG)—has undergone a radical transformation, redefining itself from a traditional equity exchange into a diversified, data-driven financial infrastructure powerhouse. This reinvention, accelerated since 2018 under CEO **David Schwimmer**, reflects the enduring presence of the 5Qs of Greatness: *persistence, resilience, courage, passion, and stamina.*

Persistence

LSEG's transformation didn't happen overnight. Long before it became a modern fintech leader, the Group methodically built a foundation of market infrastructure—including through its acquisitions of **FTSE Group (2011)** and later **Frank Russell Company (2014)**. These moves signaled a persistent strategy to expand beyond trading venues into **data and index services**, even when global investor attention remained fixated on IPO volume and trading fees. This strategic foresight laid the groundwork for its **landmark 2021 acquisition of Refinitiv**, a $27 billion deal that dramatically shifted LSEG's revenue model and competitive positioning[1].

Resilience

LSEG's transformation was not without challenge. The Refinitiv integration—a massive and complex undertaking—tested the Group's operational and cultural agility. Despite factors including the COVID-19 pandemic, political uncertainty post-Brexit shifting regulatory regimes, LSEG remained focused The Group has delivered its integration targets, accelerated growth and is consistently delivering strong shareholder returns – a credit to the strength of LSEG's 'all weather' business model.

Moreover, the transformation of the Group has continued at pace, including the successful exit of the 37 per cent economic stake held by a Blackstone led consortium. The transaction, which defied expectations, placed at a premium and remains one of the most successful and largest ever exits from a stake in a European corporate.

Courage

The decision to acquire Refinitiv and pivot LSEG's identity required significant courage. The move was met with skepticism by analysts and investors who questioned whether a centuries-old exchange could reinvent itself as a modern data and analytics leader. LSEG doubled down, forging a **10-year strategic partnership with Microsoft**, integrating **Dow Jones brands** alongside Reuters into its new **Workspace platform**, and investing deeply in cloud technology[4]. Courage was also evident in LSEG's ongoing efforts to defend and modernize London's capital markets—even as some companies considered U.S. listings and critics declared the "death" of the London IPO market[5].

Passion

Though often perceived as a measured institution, LSEG's internal transformation reveals a culture driven by passion for innovation. Its leadership envisions a future where data—not just trading—is the core utility of global finance. Launching **LSEG Workspace**, and embedding **AI** into its product strategy reflect a passionate commitment to shaping the next generation of market intelligence. This intellectual curiosity and hunger for relevance have attracted top talent in technology, economics, and data science to join its ranks.

Stamina

If one trait defines LSEG's recent success, it's stamina. Reinventing a legacy business while navigating geopolitical shifts, digital disruption, and public scrutiny requires more than vision—it demands endurance. LSEG has stayed the course through the multi-year Refinitiv integration, evolving client expectations, and the pressure to perform as a publicly listed, globally watched institution. Even as public attention drifts to tech unicorns and

U.S. exchanges, LSEG's continued evolution proves it is built not just to compete—but to endure.

I have worked with the current LSEG leadership team for several years. They are seriously focused on delivering results and innovating. The story of LSEG is no longer just about the movement of capital. It is now a case study in **adaptive greatness**—driven by strategic persistence, executed with resilience, fueled by courage, sustained by passion, and proven through stamina. In reshaping its identity, LSEG has reaffirmed its role at the center of global markets—not just as a marketplace, but as a modern infrastructure well positioned to drive change across financial markets.

In Organizations, the 5Qs Can Be Cultural Pillars

Goldman Sachs and the London Stock Exchange Group are, at first glance, two very different institutions—one a storied American investment bank, born in the nineteenth century, the other a centuries-old exchange now transformed into a modern data and analytics powerhouse. Yet, when viewed through the lens of the *Greatness Code*, both organizations reveal something deeper: Enduring success is built not simply on strategy or capital, but also on the character of the people who lead, adapt, and persevere. The 5Qs—persistence, resilience, courage, passion, and stamina—are not just traits found in extraordinary individuals; they are the lifeblood of institutions that transcend their original mandates and rise to global relevance across generations.

Consider the arc of Goldman Sachs. From Marcus Goldman's immigrant journey as founder in 1869, to the firm's modern-day navigation of financial crises and global expansion, the story is one of relentless persistence and calculated risk-taking. Equally compelling is LSEG's transformation. Once seen primarily as a national exchange, it now serves as one of the world's most influential providers of financial market infrastructure and data, thanks to visionary leadership, bold acquisitions, and a clear commitment to digital reinvention. Both firms had to navigate complex environments—Goldman through the volatility of global finance, and LSEG through the rapidly shifting world of data, regulation, and geopolitics. Both succeeded not because they were immune to failure, but because they were equipped with the internal culture and leadership mindset to evolve.

This is the essence of the *Greatness Code*. Greatness is not confined to a moment in time or a spike in performance—it's the sustained ability to confront change with intention. It requires resilience when your foundation is shaken, courage when the road forward is uncharted, and stamina to continue when others stop. Goldman Sachs and LSEG are institutional mirrors of these principles. They show us that success is not a static achievement but a dynamic journey that demands reinvention, integrity, and grit at every level of the enterprise.

As you reflect on your own path—whether as a leaders in the building trades or other vocations, or as an executive, entrepreneur, student, or someone navigating a career pivot—the stories of Goldman Sachs and LSEG offer more than inspiration. They offer a framework for you as an individual and as a leader. Ask yourself: Are you cultivating the persistence to stay the course, even when the rewards are uncertain? Are you building the resilience to bounce back—and bounce forward—when things don't go as planned? Are you leading with passion, acting with courage, and investing in the stamina to go the distance?

The Greatness Code is not a theory—it's a lived reality. These institutions prove that when the 5Qs are embedded into culture and character alike, extraordinary outcomes follow. Your story may not be written on the walls of a global exchange or trading floor, but it can be no less powerful. Because greatness—real, enduring greatness—isn't about where you begin. It's about what you build, who you become, and how hard you are willing to work. Go for it! I hope these pages have shown you that your Greatness is within your ultimate control. You can persist and move ahead in the face of challenges. You can pivot when that's the right move to make. You can courageously make things happen if you build the courage muscle. Your present and your future are YOURS.

Epilogue

The Brain's Evolution: From Striving to Thriving as You Come Down the Mountain

To finish strong, we must shift our focus from personal achievement to lifting others up. This is how we make our greatest contribution.
—Arthur Brooks, *From Strength to Strength*

In his book, *From Strength to Strength*, Arthur Brooks brilliantly explores how our mental and emotional capabilities evolve over time, and how true fulfillment comes not from clinging to the strengths of youth, but from embracing the wisdom of maturity.

I saw him present on this topic live during a fabulous keynote presentation he made at the Futures Industry Association conference in 2025. My friend Frank LaSalla, CEO of DTCC, hosted the lunch where Arthur presented. Arthur argues that persistence, resilience, and courage are not fixed traits, but mental muscles that grow stronger when we embrace the natural cognitive transformation from fluid intelligence to crystallized intelligence. They are capacities that deepen as we shift from one kind of intelligence to another.

The Shift from Fluid to Crystallized Intelligence

According to Arthur, our early careers are powered by fluid intelligence—the quick-thinking, innovative ability to solve novel problems. But as we age, this naturally declines. What rises in its place is crystallized intelligence—the capacity to synthesize knowledge, teach, mentor, and see patterns. This shift, in my view, allows for deeper persistence and resilience, because we're no longer chasing speed—we're embracing wisdom.

He notes, "Your professional decline is coming (sooner than you think). But this turns out to be good news—if you understand it, accept it, and take action." Arthur argues that many people suffer emotionally and spiritually because they resist this transition. Clearly, this can surface as people face retirement. But those who accept and even welcome it are the ones who find greater courage and clarity. This shift actually makes us more emotionally stable. He taught me in his lecture that we become better at pattern recognition, less reactive, and more grounded—key ingredients for sustained persistence and calm courage.

Courage Comes from Clarity, Not Control

Arthur notes that people often confuse courage with fearlessness. But true courage emerges when we confront the inevitability of change and loss—and choose to grow anyway. This is especially true in midlife and beyond, when the brain's priorities shift toward meaning and service. Arthur shows that true courage isn't feeling zero fear amid uncertainty—it's the quiet strength to face change with a clear mind and open heart. He again notes this requires actively engaging the prefrontal cortex (by focusing on conscious decision-making), which helps to disengage from the amygdala's fight-or-flight reactivity.

> Happiness is not a feeling—it's a decision, a habit, and a practice. It is also a skill we can develop through conscious effort.
> —Arthur Brooks, *Build the Life You Want*

By training ourselves to focus on meaning, connection, and contribution, we condition our brain to respond to uncertainty with curiosity, not fear. That is the foundation of courage. In essence, the brain rewires itself toward legacy and love. This rewiring—when embraced—becomes the source of courage to face uncertainty, aging, and even mortality.

Persistence Comes from Passion, Not Pressure

Arthur's research notes that later in life, we persist not because we're being pushed by competition, but because we're pulled by conviction. He describes this as the "second curve" of success, where passion becomes internalized and enduring. To paraphrase, he emphasizes that success is not about never giving up; it's about knowing what's worth giving yourself to. Purpose once again is an important theme. It's the shift to applying your passion toward a purpose. He teaches that this shift activates different neural pathways—moving from dopamine-driven reward circuits to more serotonin and oxytocin-based systems tied to trust, connection, and inner calm. This form of persistence is sustainable, because it draws from intrinsic motivation—the desire to serve, to love, to create legacy—not external validation.

Building Resilience through Letting Go

One of his most powerful insights is that satisfaction comes not from holding on, but from learning to let go—of ego, status, and outdated definitions of success. Put another way, we become more resilient when we detach our identity from external achievement and ground it instead in purpose and connection.

> "The key to deep happiness is not success, but purpose."

Arthur emphasizes that much of our suffering comes from clinging to who we used to be. Resilience, he says, comes not from refusing to change, but from letting go with grace—of ego, identity, and past measures of success.

> "Happiness requires letting go of our attachments to things that decay—and instead leaning into love, relationships, and purpose."

Arthur says that by consciously using the more reflective and empathetic parts of our brain—the prefrontal cortex and areas associated with emotional regulation—we build what he calls "metacognitive awareness." This means we can step back from negative thoughts, see them for what they are, and choose a better response. Resilience, then, is not just the ability to endure hardship. It's the ability to reframe hardship as meaningful. This is a cognitive and spiritual shift that happens when we stop living for performance and start living for contribution.

A True Story of These Principals in Action: Tom Perna

My first mentor on Wall Street was Tom Perna. He was a hard-charging senior executive at The Bank of New York. He helped the bank navigate the devastating World Trade Center attack and the technical challenges that followed, which literally keep the world's financial markets functioning.

To fully appreciate the magnitude of this example of making the mental shift, you need some context. Tom grew up on the streets of Brooklyn, New York. Never went to college, but at a very young age, achieved major career success on Wall Street. Many saw him as intimidating. He was tough. By the way, he was a super leader, tough, but empathetic. That combination was not common among leaders at the time.

After retiring, he was pursued by another major financial institution that wanted him to come out of retirement. I love this story, and it embodies so much of what Arthur Brooks teaches. They invited him to meet. He had begun to serve on corporate boards, so the invitation was not out of the ordinary. However, when he arrived, they quickly explained that they wanted him to come out of retirement and take a major executive job with their organization. Tom had retired young, in his 50s. His answer illustrates Arthur's thesis. They said to him, "We really want you here." He said, "No, you don't." They pressed him and said, "We really do." He again said, "no you don't." They pressed again. That's when he finally made his point. He said, "No you don't. You want the guy I used to be. . ." I tell people all the time, Tom was never one of those people who called me for help after retirement. He didn't need it. He made the shift in every way. When he walked out of that bank, he didn't need his corporate title, or power, or any of those legacy pieces. He had moved on. Not easily done.

In Conclusion: Using the Brain to Stay Positive

Arthur ultimately argues that our brain becomes better equipped for deep persistence, resilience, and courage as we age—if we allow it. These aren't just heroic traits; they're byproducts of a profound internal shift toward wisdom, purpose, and spiritual maturity. On page 96 in his book, *Strength to Strength*, Arthur tells us "If you want to finish life strong, you must make the leap from being a striver to being a teacher and a giver."

Arthur blends neuroscience, psychology, and philosophy to teach us how to stay positive—not by denying decline, but by embracing the strengths that come with it. He urges us to:

- Shift attention from novelty to meaning, using the prefrontal cortex to reflect and reframe.
- Quiet the amygdala, the area of our brain responsible for fear, by focusing on gratitude and service.
- Cultivate habits like meditation and prayer, which change brain structure and enhance emotional control.
- Practice detachment from ego, drawing on the parts of the brain associated with empathy and long-term perspective.

As we age, we have a choice: Resist change and suffer, or embrace evolution and thrive. According to Arthur, the brain is wired for renewal—if we use it wisely.

As we have learned throughout this book, persistence, resilience, and courage are not just traits to admire. They are three of the *Greatness Code*'s five pillars, which we can build by training the mind to focus on what truly matters. Arthur Brooks explains this beautifully.

Now, after 40, 50, 60, or 70 years of work, you have touched many people. Hopefully, most in a positive way. Empathy for yourself and others is the key to a life well lived. *Godspeed to you on your journey.*

Proceed to GreatnessCode.com for More Insights

Bibliography

Abad-Santos, A. "Simone Biles's Legacy Is Equal Parts Dominance and Resilience." *Vox*, August 1, 2024, vox.com/culture/363796/simone-biles-gold-medal-team-final-2024-olympics-result.

Adams-Earley, C. (1996). *One Woman's Army: A Black Officer Remembers the WAC*, Illustratede. Texas A&M University Press.

Alder, S.L. (2013). *300 Questions to Ask Your Parents Before It's Too Late*. Cedar Fort.

Alexander, C. Interviewed by the author, circa 2020.

Alley-Young, G. (2013). Jackley, Jessica. In: *The Multimedia Encyclopedia of Women in Today's World*, vol. 1 (ed. M.Z. Stange, C.K. Oyster, and J.E. Sloan), 964–967. Sage Publications.

Amazon.com, Inc. "Amazon 2024 Annual Report." Amazon Investor Relations, 2025, https://s2.q4cdn.com/299287126/files/doc_financials/2025/ar/Amazon-2024-Annual-Report.pdf.

Angelou, M. (1993). *Wouldn't Take Nothing for My Journey Now*. Bantam.

Antwi, J. and Naanwaab, C.B. (2022). Generational differences, risk tolerance, and ownership of financial securities: Evidence from the United States. *International Journal of Financial Studies* 10 (2): article 35. MDPI. https://doi.org/10.3390/ijfs10020035.

Arington, B. Interviewed by the author, April 2025.

Atkins, B. (2019). *Be Board Ready: The Secrets to Landing a Board Seat and Being a Great Director*. Ideapress Publishing.

Bandura, A. (1977). *Social Learning Theory*. Prentice-Hall.

Bezos, J. (2011). In Conversation with Jeff Bezos: CEO of the Internet. *Wired* 12.

Bilton, N. (2014). *Hatching Twitter: A True Story of Money, Power, Friendship, and Betrayal*. Portfolio.

Bloomberg News. "Goldman Adapts to Market Pressure with New Strategy Shift." *Bloomberg.com*, March 2023.

Bradt, G., Check, J.A., and Lawler, J.A. (2022). *The New Leader's 100-Day Action Plan: Take Charge, Build Your Team, and Deliver Better Results Faster*, 5th Edition. Wiley.

British Council Corporate Insights. *Gen Z in the Workplace: Bridging the Soft Skills Gap to Drive Success*. June 2023, corporate.britishcouncil.org/insights/gen-z-workplace-bridging-soft-skills-gap-drive-success.

Bourne, E. Collaborated on text with Author on LSEG content. July 2025.

Brooks, A.C. (2022). *From Strength to Strength: Finding Success, Happiness, and Deep Purpose in the Second Half of Life*. Portfolio.

Brooks, A. et al. (2008). Volunteering, self-reported health and happiness: International evidence from 66 Countries. *Social Science & Medicine* 66 (11): 2321–2334.

Bryant, K. (2018). *The Mamba Mentality: How I Play*. MCD.

Bryant, K. "Mamba Mentality: Kobe Bryant's Words of Wisdom." Religion of Sports, May 15, 2021, https://www.youtube.com/watch?v=ym-o65Dub8c.

Buffett, W.E. (1976). Benjamin Graham (1894–1976). *Financial Analysts Journal* 32 (6): 19–20. https://doi.org/10.2469/faj.v32.n6.19.

Burnison, G. (2021). *The Five Graces of Life and Leadership*. Wiley.

Butler, R.A. "Putting Sustainability at the Center of Business Strategy: An Interview with Paul Polman." *Mongabay*, October 13, 2020, news.mongabay.com/2020/10/putting-sustainability-at-the-center-of-business-strategy-an-interview-with-paul-polman.

Casolino, D. Interviewed by the author, April 2025.

Center for Creative Leadership. "The Importance of Empathy in the Workplace." April 28, 2024, www.ccl.org/articles/leading-effectively-articles/empathy-in-the-workplace-a-tool-for-effective-leadership.

Chernow, R. (1990). *The House of Morgan: An American Banking Dynasty and the Rise of Modern Finance*. Grove Press.

Churchill Archive Centre. "Margaret Thatcher: A Biography." n.d., https://archives.chu.cam.ac.uk/collections/thatcher-papers/thatcher-biography/.

Churchill, W.S. (1974). *Winston Churchill: His Complete Speeches, 1897–1963*, vol. 7 (ed. R.R. James). Chelsea House Publishers.

Churchill, W.S. (1949). *Their Finest Hour*, vol. 2, 521. Cassell & Co.

Claassen, C. *Tennessee Whiskey: The Dean Dillon Story*, 2017.

Coger, B. "Legendary Country Songwriter Dean Dillon Talks About Writing Classic Hit Songs for George Strait, Toby Keith, and Kenny Chesney." *Songwriter Universe*, 2013, www.songwriteruniverse.com/dean-dillon-123/?utm.

Cohan, W.D. (2011). *Money and Power: How Goldman Sachs Came to Rule the World*. Doubleday.

Corcoran, B. Interviewed by the author, circa 2007. Also quoted in Guarino (2007). *Smart Is Not Enough*. Wiley.

Country Music Hall of Fame. "Dean Dillon," n.d., www.countrymusichalloffame.org/hall-of-fame/dean-dillon.

Dailyhistory.org. "Why Was Margaret Thatcher Called the Iron Lady," n.d., https://www.dailyhistory.org/Why_was_Margaret_Thatcher_called_the_Iron_Lady.

Daly, R. Interviewed by the author, 2010 through 2025.

Deloitte. "2025 Gen Z and Millennial Survey." *Deloitte Insights*, May 2025, www.deloitte.com/global/en/issues/work/genz-millennial-survey.html.

Deloitte. "Gen Zs and Millennials at Work: Pursuing a Balance of Money, Meaning, and Well-Being." *Deloitte Insights*, June 2, 2025, www.deloitte.com/us/en/insights/topics/talent/2025-gen-z-millennial-survey.html.

Deloitte. "Making Waves: How Gen Zs and Millennials Are Prioritizing—and Driving—Change in the Workplace." *Deloitte Insights*, May 2023, www.deloitte.com/us/en/insights/topics/talent/recruiting-gen-z-and-millennials.html.

Denning, S. "Former Unilever CEO Paul Polman Says Aiming for Sustainability Isn't Good Enough—The Goal Is Much Higher." *Harvard Business Review*, November 19, 2021, hbr.org/2021/11/former-unilever-ceo-paul-polman-says-aiming-for-sustainability-isnt-good-enough-the-goal-is-much-higher.

Diamond, A. (2013). Executive functions. *Annual Review of Psychology* 64 (1): 135–168. https://doi.org/10.1146/annurev-psych-113011-143750.

Dillon, D. Interviewed by the author, October 2024 and May 2025.

DeMeuse, K.P. (n.d.). *What's Smarter Than IQ? Learning Agility*. The Korn Ferry Institute, www.kornferry.com/content/dam/kornferry/docs/pdfs/whats-smarter-than-iq-learning-agility.pdf.

Doran, G.T. (1981). There's a S.M.A.R.T. Way to Write Management's Goals and Objectives. *Management Review*, https://community.mis.temple.edu/mis0855002fall2015/files/2015/10/S.M.A.R.T-Way-Management-Review.pdf.

Duckworth, A. (2018). *Grit: The Power of Passion and Perseverance*. Scribner.

Dweck, C.S. (2006). *Mindset: The New Psychology of Success*. Random House Gerber.

Ellis, C.D. (2008). *The Partnership: The Making of Goldman Sachs*. Penguin Press.

Eskreis-Winkler, L., Duckworth, A.L., Shulman, E.P., and Beal, S.A. (2014). The grit effect: Predicting retention in the military, the workplace, school and marriage. *Frontiers in Psychology 5*: 36. https://doi.org/10.3389/fpsyg.2014.00036.

Ford Newsroom. "Alan Mulally." n.d., https://media.ford.com/content/fordmedia/fna/us/en/people/alan-mulally.html.

Fox, L. Interviewed by the author, circa 2009 through May 2025.

Frankel, G. "'I Fight On,' Thatcher Declares." *The Washington Post*, November 22, 1990, https://www.washingtonpost.com/archive/politics/1990/11/22/i-fight-on-thatcher-declares/ed0eeecb-ec76-46e3-b489-adc42dbcc5cc/.

Free From Burnout. "How Gen X Burnout Differs From Other Generations." 2022, www.freefromburnout.com/blog-1/how-genx-burnout-differs-from-other-generations.

Freshfields Bruckhaus Deringer. "LSEG and Microsoft Launch Strategic Partnership." December 2022, https://www.freshfields.com.

Financial News London. "LSEG Posts Strong 2024 Results, Boosts Buyback." March 2024.

Fry, R. and Aragão, C. "Gender Pay Gap in U.S. Has Narrowed Slightly Over 2 Decades." *Pew Research Center*, March 4, 2025, www.pewresearch.org/short-reads/2025/03/04/gender-pay-gap-in-us-has-narrowed-slightly-over-2-decades/.

FundingUniverse. "History of the Goldman Sachs Group Inc." n.d., www.fundinguniverse.com/company-histories/the-goldman-sachs-group-inc-history/.

Bibliography

Gabler, N. (2006). *Walt Disney: The Triumph of the American Imagination*. Alfred A. Knopf.

Gerber, S. and Paugh, R. (2018). *Superconnector: Stop Networking and Start Building Business Relationships That Matter*. Balance.

Gerstner, L. (2003). *Who Says Elephants Can't Dance?* Harper Business.

Girls Who Code. (n.d.). "We're on a Mission to Close the Gender Gap in Tech." https://girlswhocode.com/about-us.

Gladwell, M. (2008). *Outliers: The Story of Success*. Little, Brown.

Goldman Sachs. *Annual Reports*, 2000–2020.

Goldman Sachs. "Entrepreneurialism and Grit Inspire Marcus Goldman to Launch his Business." n.d., www.goldmansachs.com/our-firm/history/moments/1869-founding-of-gs.

Goldman Sachs. "Firm's First IPO Uses New Earnings-Based Approach to Valuation." n.d., www.goldmansachs.com/our-firm/history/moments/1906-united-cigar.

Goldman Sachs. "Goldman Sachs Announces It Will Become a Bank Holding Company." n.d., www.goldmansachs.com/our-firm/history/moments/2008-bank-holding-company.

Goldman Sachs. "Goldman Sachs to Repurchase TARP Preferred Stock." 9 June 2009, www.goldmansachs.com/pressroom/press-releases/2009/june-9-release.

Goldman Sachs. "In a Paradigm Shift, Goldman Sachs Decides to Go Public." n.d., www.goldmansachs.com/our-firm/history/moments/1999-ipo.

Goldman Sachs. "Sidney Weinberg Leads the Firm for More than Three Decades." n.d., www.goldmansachs.com/our-firm/history/moments/1930-sidney-weinberg-leads.

Goleman, D. "Empathy A Key to Effective Leadership." LinkedIn, June 7, 2017, www.linkedin.com/pulse/empathy-key-effective-leadership-daniel-goleman/.

Gorman, J. Collaborated on text with the author, February 2025.

Grant, A. (2013). *Give and Take: A Revolutionary Approach to Success*. Viking Press.

Graziosi, D. Interviewed by the author, circa 1991 through May 2025.

Grove, A. (1996). *Only the Paranoid Survive: How to Exploit the Crisis Points That Challenge Every Company*. Doubleday.

Guarino, A.C. (2007). *Smart Is Not Enough: The South Pole Strategy and Other Powerful Talent Management Secrets*. Wiley.

Harmony Healthcare IT. "State of Gen Z Mental Health 2025." 2025, harmonyhit.com/state-of-gen-z-mental-health/.

Harvard Business School Executive Education – Board Programs. n.d., www.exed.hbs.

Harris, C. Collaborated on text with Author, June 2025.

Harris, C.A. (2010). *Expect to Win: Proven Strategies for Success from a Wall Street Vet*. Hudson Street Press.

Harris C. "Meet Carla," n.d., https://www.carlaspearls.com/about.

Hoffman, R., Casnocha, B., and Yeh, C. (2014). *The Start-Up of You: Adapt to the Future, Invest in Yourself, and Transform Your Career*. Crown Business.

Huffington, A. (2014). *Thrive: The Third Metric to Redefining Success and Creating a Life of Well-Being, Wisdom, and Wonder*. Harmony Books.

Hornsby, A. "Clifford L. Alexander, Jr. (1933–2022)." *BlackPast*, 20 May 2007, https://www.blackpast.org/african-american-history/alexander-clifford-l-jr-1933/.

Islam, S. Collaborated on text with the author, June 2025.

Islam, S. "My Story." Accessed June 6, 2025, https://www.sabirulislam.com/my-story/.

Jackley, J. "Clay Water Brick: Finding inspiration from entrepreneurs who do the most with the least", 2015.

Jurek, S. "Scott Jurek, Ultramarathoner: Living for the Run." *Conscious Connection Magazine*, 2016, www.consciousconnectionmagazine.com/2016/08/scott-jurek-interview/. Accessed July 20, 2025.

Jurek, S. "What Vegan Ultrarunner Scott Jurek Likes to Eat." *Bon Appétit*, 2016, www.bonappetit.com/people/article/scott-jurek-ultrarunner-diet. Accessed July 20, 2025.

Kennerley, M. "Dean Dillon: Living the Lyrics." *BMI MusicWorld*, 2011, https://www.bmi.com/news/entry/20070213dean_dillon_living_the_lyrics.

Kilpatrick, A. (2007). *Of Permanent Value: The Story of Warren Buffett*. Andy Kilpatrick Publishing Empire.

Kim, E. "Marc Benioff's Routine: 8 Hours Sleep, Meditation." *Business Insider*, June 15, 2024, www.businessinsider.com/salesforce-marc-benioff-comments-on-meditation-sleep-schedule-2023.

Kim, E. "Salesforce Put Meditation Rooms on Every Floor of Its New Tower." *Business Insider*, March 7, 2016.

Bibliography

Kim, S., Halvorsen, C., Potter, C., and Faul, J. (2024). Does volunteering reduce epigenetic age acceleration among retired and working older adults? Results from the Health and Retirement Study. *Social Science & Medicine* 364: 117501. https://doi.org/10.1016/j.socscimed.2024.117501.

Knudsen, E.I. (2004). Sensitive periods in the development of the brain and behavior. *Journal of Cognitive Neuroscience* 16 (8): 1412–1425. https://doi.org/10.1162/0898929042304796.

Korn Ferry. (2018). *March to Equality: Advancing Women Worldwide*. Korn Ferry, www.kornferry.com/insights/this-week-in-leadership/advancing-women-worldwide-leadership-2018.

Korn Ferry. "Enhancing Learning Agility through Coaching." n.d., www.kornferry.com/capabilities/talent-suite-hcm-software/korn-ferry-assess/learning-agility-tools.

Krueger, J. "Millennials Are Seeing Their Net Worth Go Down." *Forbes*, March 17, 2023, forbes.com/sites/julietkrueger/2023/03/17/student-loans-impact-on-millennial-net-worth-the-importance-of-strategic-college-financing/.

Lacy, B.A. "A Community Grows Its Way out of Poverty." *Faith & Leadership*, October 6, 2015.

LaMotte, S. S. "Forget Millennials. Gen Xers Are the Future of Work." *Time*, October 2, 2014, time.com/3456522/millennials-generation-x-work.

Lane, R. "Warren Buffett's $50 Billion Decision." *Forbes*, March 26, 2012, www.forbes.com/sites/randalllane/2012/03/26/warren-buffetts-50-billion-decision/.

Leblanc, R. (2020). *The Handbook of Board Governance: A Comprehensive Guide for Public, Private, and Not-for-Profit Board Members*, 2nde. Wiley.

Lewis, M. (2010). *The Big Short: Inside the Doomsday Machine*. W. W. Norton & Company.

Li, Y. and Wang, J. (2024). Individual social capital and career expectations: Evidence from Australia. *The Economic and Labour Relations Review* 35 (1): 52–70. https://doi.org/10.1177/10353046241234145.

London Stock Exchange Group. "LSEG Completes Acquisition of Refinitiv." January 29, 2021, https://www.lseg.com.

London Stock Exchange Group. "LSEG 2024 Preliminary Results." March 1, 2024.

Martin, L. Collaborated on text with Author, May 2025.

Martin, M. "Walt Disney Didn't Actually Draw Mickey Mouse. Meet the Kansas City Artist Who Did." NPR, July 7, 2021, https://news.azpm.org/p/news-npr/2021/7/7/197019-walt-disney-didnt-actually-draw-mickey-mouse-meet-the-kansas-city-artist-who-did/.

Mäthner, E. and Lanwehr, R. "Givers, takers and matchers – Reciprocity styles and their contribution to organizational behaviour". *Gruppe. Interaktion. Organisation (GIO)*, 2017, https://www.researchgate.net/publication/313788094_Givers_takers_and_matchers_-_Reciprocity_styles_and_their_contribution_to_organizational_behaviour

Matsangou, E. "Unilever CEO Paul Polman Is Redefining Sustainable Business." *European CEO*, 2022, www.europeanceo.com/business-and-management/unilever-ceo-paul-polman-is-redefining-sustainable-business/.

Maxwell, J.C. (2001). *The 17 Indisputable Laws of Teamwork: Embrace Them and Empower Your Team*. Thomas Nelson.

McGeehan, P. "Goldman's Strategy Shifts." *The New York Times*, September 2008.

McGough, N.B. "80 Retirement Quotes That Will Resonate With Any Retiree." *Southern Living*, November 21, 2024, https://www.southernliving.com/culture/retirement-quotes.

McRaven, W.H. University of Texas at Austin Commencement Address, May 17, 2014, 19 min, 26 sec.

Miller, G.E., Chen, E., and Zhou, E.S. (2007). If it goes up, must it come down? Chronic stress and the hypothalamic–pituitary–adrenocortical axis in humans. *Psychological Bulletin* 133 (1): 25–45. https://doi.org/10.1037/0033-2909.133.1.25.

Millstein, I.M. (1998). *Corporate Governance: Improving Competitiveness and Access to Capital in Global Markets*. OECD.

Meichenbaum, D. (1985). *Stress Inoculation Training*. Pergamon Press.

Moms First. "Moms First Summit Makes History: Thousands of Moms Come Together to Finish the Fight for Gender Equality." *Moms First*, May 17, 2024, momsfirst.us/news/momsfirstsummit/.

Mentoring Resource Center. *Who Mentored You? Exploring Mentoring Experiences Across Generations*. MRC/Mentor, January 2023, www.mentoring.org/wp-content/uploads/2023/01/Who-Mentored-You.pdf.

Moultrie, R. Interviewed by the author, February 2025 through May 2025.

Bibliography

Mulally, A. and Witty, A. (2021). *Relentless Implementation: Creating Clarity, Alignment and a Working Together Operating System to Maximize Your Business Performance*. Forbes Books.

Nashville Songwriters Hall of Fame. "Dean Dillon." n.d., https://nashvillesongwritersfoundation.com/Site/inductee?entry_id=4124.

National Museum U.S. Army. "A Different Kind of Victory: The 6888th Central Postal Directory Battalion." n.d., www.thenmusa.org/articles/a-different-kind-of-victory-the-6888th-central-postal-directory-battalion.

Neff, K. (2018). *The Mindful Self-Compassion Workbook: A Proven Way to Accept Yourself, Build Inner Strength, and Thrive*. Guilford Press.

Sananka, O., Katumpe, G., and Kyongo, J.K. (2023). Millennials' Workplace Challenges and Global Market. *International Journal of Academic Research in Business and Social Sciences* 4 (3).

Schwimmer, D. (2024). *How to Save London's Stock Market*. The Times (UK).

Papadatou, A. "Why are Millennials dubbed as the most impatient generation in the workplace?" HRreview.co.uk, February 19, 2019, https://hrreview.co.uk/hr-news/why-are-millennials-dubbed-as-the-most-impatient-generation-in-the-workplace/114928.

Pappas, C. Interviewed by the author, circa 2010 through June 2025.

Pappas, J. Interviewed by the author, circa 2010 through June 2025.

Perna, T. Collaborated on text with Author, July 2025.

Perry, T. *The Six Triple Eight*, Netflix, 2024, www.netflix.com/title/81590591.

Playback.fm. "Top 100 Country Songs in 1978." n.d., https://playback.fm/charts/country/1978illboard.

Pollak, L. "Gen X, The Forgotten Middle Child. . ." 2020, lindseypollak.com/gen-x-the-forgotten-middle-child-theme-song.

Polman, P. and Bhattacharya, C.B. "Engaging Employees to Create a Sustainable Business." *Stanford Social Innovation Review*, Fall 2016, ssir.org/articles/entry/engaging_employees_to_create_a_sustainable_business.

Raddon, H.A.M. "Gen X: The 'Middle Child' Generation! Unhappy, Unprepared and Overlooked?" *Raddon Report*, March 30, 2023, www.raddon.com/en/insights/raddon_report/gen-x-middle-child.html.

Ramsay, G., Sinnott, J., and Wright, R. "'I Have to Focus on my Mental Health,' Says Simone Biles after Withdrawing from Gold Medal Event." *CNN*, July 29, 2021, www.cnn.com/2021/07/27/sport/simone-biles-tokyo-2020-olympics.

Ransom, D. "Barbara Corcoran: Forget Balance, I Strive for Anti-Exhaustion." *Inc.*, November 10, 2014, www.inc.com/diana-ransom/why-martha-stewart-and-barbara-corcoran-dont-believe-in-work-life-balance.html.

Reagan, R. "We who live in free market societies believe that growth, prosperity and, ultimately, human fulfillment are created from the bottom up, not the government down." Speech, September 29, 1981, https://www.reaganfoundation.org/ronald-reagan/quotes/we-who-live-in-free-market-societies-believe-that?srsltid=AfmBOori_yfLJziQQ4M-0hXwPjIBnXqL647k_Hp7y7M5LQosOczRYZke&utm.

Rolet, X. Interviewed by the author, August 2025.

Rowling, J.K. "J.K. Rowling on Failure." Harvard Commencement Speech, 2008, 7 min, 32 sec. www.youtube.com/watch?v=QA4clU4iw1U.

Rungo, P., Sánchez-Santos, J.M., and Pena-López, A. (2024). Individual social capital and expectations of career advancement. *The Economic and Labour Relations Review* 35 (1): 118–139. https://doi.org/10.1017/elr.2024.3.

Saujana, R. Collaborated on text with Author May, 2025.

Seery, M.D., Holman, E.A., and Silver, R.C. (2010). Whatever does not kill us: Cumulative lifetime adversity, vulnerability, and resilience. *Journal of Personality and Social Psychology* 99 (6): 1025–1041. https://doi.org/10.1037/a0021344.

Segal, E. "Why the Social and Verbal Skills of Some Gen Z Workers Have Declined." *Forbes*, June 16, 2024, www.forbes.com/sites/edwardsegal/2024/06/16/why-the-social-and-verbal-skills-of-some-gen-z-workers-have-declined/.

Sengupta, S., Perlroth, N., and Wortham, J., "Instagram's Founders Were Helped by Bay Area Connections." *The New York Times*, April 14, 2012, https://www.nytimes.com/2012/04/14/technology/instagram-founders-were-helped-by-bay-area-connections.html.

Sorkin, A.R. (2009). *Too Big to Fail: The Inside Story of How Wall Street and Washington Fought to Save the Financial System—and Themselves*. Viking.

Bibliography

Speaking.com. "Kevin Systrom." n.d., https://speaking.com/speakers/kevin-systrom.

Sprecher, J. Interviewed by the author, July 2025.

Statista. "Annual Revenue of Amazon Web Services (AWS) from 2013 to 2024." n.d., www.statista.com/statistics/233725/development-of-amazon-web-services-revenue/.

Sterling, T. "Dean Dillon Biography." *AllMusic*, n.d., www.allmusic.com/artist/dean-dillon-mn0000226643#biography.

Stevenson, J. E. and Orr, E. "We Interviewed 57 Female CEOs to Find Out How More Women Can Get to the Top." *Harvard Business Review*, November 8, 2017. Harvard Business Publishing, https://hbr.org/2017/11/we-interviewed-57-female-ceos-to-find-out-how-more-women-can-get-to-the-top.

Stevenson, J. and Orr, E. "What Makes Women CEOs Different?" Korn Ferry, November 8, 2017, www.kornferry.com/insights/this-week-in-leadership/women-ceo-insights.

Stone, B. (2013). *The Everything Store: Jeff Bezos and the Age of Amazon*. Little, Brown and Company.

Saujani, R. Interviewed by the author, May 2025.

Talker Research. "Quarter of Americans Experience Burnout Before They're 30." *Talker Research*, March 11, 2025, talker.news/2025/03/11/quarter-of-americans-experience-burnout-by-30/.

Taylor, P. and Gao, G. "Generation X: America's Neglected 'Middle Child.'" Pew Research Center, June 5, 2014, www.pewresearch.org/short-reads/2014/06/05/generation-x-americas-neglected-middle-child/.

Tenore, H. and Jackson, S. "Salesforce CEO Marc Benioff Says He Gets Around 8 Hours of Sleep a Night and Starts Every Morning the Same Way." *Business Insider*, June 15, 2024, www.businessinsider.com/salesforce-marc-benioff-comments-on-meditation-sleep-schedule-2023-11.

Thomas, B. "Solving the Mystery of Millennial and Gen Z Job Hoppers." *Business News Daily*, 2023, www.businessnewsdaily.com/7012-millennial-job-hopping.html.

Today.com. "Ariana Huffington: Collapse from Exhaustion Was a 'Wake-up Call.'" n.d., Today.com, www.today.com/health/arianna-huffington-collapse-exhaustion-was-wake-call-2d79644042.

Unal, A. "Simone Biles Says She Was 'a Lot Happier' at Paris 2024 Than Previous Olympics: 'It's Pure Joy.'" *People*, 6 Aug. 2024, people.com/simone-biles-happier-paris-2024-than-previous-olympics-8690752.

U.S. Army Center of Military History. *Secretaries of War and Secretaries of the Army: Portraits and Biographical Sketches, 1789–2021*. U.S. Department of the Army, 2021, https://history.army.mil/html/books/secretariesofwar/.

Vince, R. Interviewed by the author, July 2025.

Walt Disney Family Museum. "Ub Iwerks: Master of Animation and Technology." n.d., www.waltdisney.org/blog/ub-iwerks-master-animation-and-technology.

Washington, D. (2006). *A Hand to Guide Me*. Mcredith Books.

Washington, D. *The mentors he'll never forget*. Guideposts, n.d., https://guideposts.org/positive-living/the-mentors-hell-never-forget/.

Wharton School. *Givers vs. Takers: The Surprising Truth about Who Gets Ahead*. *Knowledge@Wharton*, April 10, 2013, https://knowledge.wharton.upenn.edu/podcast/knowledge-at-wharton-podcast/givers-vs-takers-the-surprising-truth-about-who-gets-ahead/.

Winarni, D.S. et al. (2023). The effect of work environment and emotional intelligence on affective commitment on millennial generation with job satisfaction as mediating variable. *Enrichment: Journal of Management* 13 (5): 3149–3162. https://doi.org/10.35335/enrichment.v13i5.1748.

Winfrey, O. quoted in Pryor, Yvonne. "I've been blessed to have Maya Angelou as my mentor, mother/sister, and friend since my 20's. She was there for me always, guiding me through some of the most . . ." Instagram, May 28, 2014, instagram.com/p/ojLc1dSS_C/?utm_source=ig_web_copy_link.

Wood, J. (2006). *Leaving Microsoft to Change the World: How One Man's Passion and Purpose Transformed an Organization and Inspired a Movement*. Free Press.

World Health Organization. "Burnout an Occupational Phenomenon: International Classification of Diseases." May 28, 2019, www.who.int/news/item/28-05-2019-burn-out-an-occupational-phenomenon-international-classification-of-diseases.

Yale Law School. "Yale Law School Mourns the Loss of Clifford L. Alexander Jr. '58." *Yale Law School*, July 5, 2022, law.yale.edu/yls-today/news/yale-law-school-mourns-loss-clifford-l-alexander-jr-58.

Index

A
Abad-Santos, Alex, 154
accountability, 62, 109
Adams, Charity, 81–82
adaptability, 121
   enduring power of, 136
   flexible mindset, 122
   legacy of, 132, 135
   strategies for, 137
   in team, 130, 131
Adecco, 10
adversity, 17, 18, 44, 108–109, 119
advisors, 46, 184
advisory board, 184, 188
advisory role, 177
   post-career, 172
agility, 18, 39
   change, 18
   learning, 18, 19
   mental, 18, 19
   people, 18, 19
   results, 18
Alexander Jr., Clifford, 141
alliances, strategic, 72–73
Alpine Strategic Partners, 29

Amazon, 121–125
Amazon Web Services (AWS), 122–125
   as Amazon's growth engine, 125
   flexibility, 123–124
   ingenuity, 123–124
   legacy of, 125
   overcoming setbacks, 124
   on unconventional path, 123
ambition, 39
   balancing, 103
   long-term impact on, 17
Andersen, Arthur, 77
Angelou, Maya, 99, 143–144
anxiety, 154
   financial, 177
   Gen Z, 25
Apple, 132, 157
Arington, Brad, 84–87
authenticity, 14, 118

B
Baby Boomers, 19–22
   community engagement, 23
   hard work, 23

balance, in career, 103
barriers, 124
    challenges overcoming, 142
    personality, 127
    racial, 143
    with relentless passion, 141
    systemic, 19
beginner's mindset, 101
Benioff, Marc, 155
Berkshire Hathaway, 56, 72
Bezos, Jeff, 121, 123–125
Biden, Joe, 128
Biles, Simone, 154
Black women, 83
BNY, xiii, xiv, xv
board
    bio and résumé, 180
    and continue learning, 182
    formal board education and certification, 181
    gain practical governance experience, 181
    interview process, 182
    level personal brand, 180
    readiness, 180
    seat, 182
    strategic network expansion, 181
    target companies, 181
BoardEx, 181
board members, 184
BoardProspects.com, 180
board role, 177
BoardStrong. org, 181
board-style résumé, 186
boundaries, 157
Bradt, George, 69
brain's reward system, 17

Branson, Richard, 100
Broadridge Financial Corporation, 77, 78
Brooks, Arthur, 197
Brown. Jim Ed, 13
Buffett, Warren, 31, 56, 72, 125
Burnison, Gary, 118
burnout, 151, 153, 157
    from dual responsibilities, Gen X, 26
    early signs of, 153
    from overcommitment, Millennials, 24
    prevention, 103, 155
    WHO definition, 153
business
    own, 171
    small, 171

C

Callahan, Tom, 105
career, 190
    early stages of, 44 (*see also* early career)
    extension, 167
    Gen Z, pragmatic decision, 25
    Millennials (Gen Y), 23
    path, 33
    peak, 23
    post-summit phase, 23
    setbacks in, 44
Carlyle Group, 114
Carter, Jimmy, 142
Casolino, Davide, 168, 169
certified financial planner (CFP), 174

Index

change
  constant, 74
  resilience through, 131–132
  societal, 20
  systemic, 8
Citi, 29
clarity, 198
coaching, 59
Cochran, Hank, 13
collaboration and trust, 13, 55, 144
commitment, 57, 63, 111
commonality, 4
community-based economies, 20
community engagement, Baby Boomers, 23
confidence, 16, 30, 62, 89, 106
conformity, 14
connection, power of, 48
connector, 68–70
consulting, 176
continual learning
  mid-career growth peak, 88
  peak-career professionals, 126
continuous growth, 121, 129
continuous learning, 119
Corcoran, Barbara, 152
Cornelius, Helen, 13
Cornell International, 113
corporate workplace, 12
country music, 14
courage, 15, 35–36, 58, 192, 194
COVID-19 pandemic, 7
  mid-career stage during, 75
creativity, 20
culture
  corporate, 74
  of resilience, 116
  workplace, 7

curiosity, 101–102
cynicism, 153

D

Daly, Richard J., 77
Darlene, 127
debt and liabilities, 173
decision-making, 18
derailers, shared, 25
Diamond, A., 18
Dillon, Dean, 13, 31
discipline, 30, 31, 34, 42
Disney, Walt, 31, 48
3D Line Medical Systems S.r.l., 169
dopamine, 17
dopamine-driven reward, 199
Dorsey, Jack, 46
Duckworth, Angela, 4–5
Duckworth equation, 4–5
due diligence advisors, 184
Dweck, Carol, 17

E

early career, 57–58
  challenges, 5
  failure as advantage, 38
  overcoming challenges, 39
  professionals, 60–63
  5 qualities, 37
  social capital, 40
early investments, 46
early-stage exercise, 59
emotional intelligence (EI), 54
  as catalyst for social capital, 55
  gaps Millennials (Gen Y), 24
emotional preparedness, 174, 175
emotional quotient (EQ), 54

emotional regulation, 18
empathy, 54, 55
   as social connector, 54
energy management, 32, 34
entrepreneurship, 177
   risks, Gen Z, 25
entry-level tech jobs, 6
Equilar BoardEdge, 181
estate planners and
      retirement plan, 178
ethical leadership, on
      legacy, 144–145
evening routines, 85, 102
executive coaching, post-career, 172
exhaustion, 153

F

failure, 12
   as advantage, 38
   embrace, 12
   healthy relationship with, 15
   reframing, 13
Falls, Nancy, 180
Federal Open Markets Committee
      (FOMC)., 73
feelings, 153
financial advisors and
      retirement plan, 178
financial anxiety, 177
financial readiness, 174
financial security, 172–173
The Five Graces of Life and Leadership
      (2021), 118
fixed mindset, 15
flexibility, Gen Z, 25
Fortune magazine, 69
Fox, Liam, 42

freelancing, 176
From Strength to Strength, 197

G

Gates, Bill, 130
Gates Foundation, 102
Gen Alpha, 22
gender pay disparities,
      Millennials, 24
generational differences, 19–23
Gen X, 19, 21, 22
   burnout from dual
      responsibilities, 26
   generalizations, 26
   limited mentorship
      opportunities, 27
   mid-career stage, 26
   overlooked by leadership, 26
   resistance to relocation, 27
   risk aversion, 26
   struggles with adaptation, 26
Gen Y *see* Millennials (Gen Y)
Gen Z, 19, 21, 22
   career, 23
   demand for flexibility, 25
   entrepreneurial risks, 25
   generalizations, 25
   greatness code in action, 51–52
   mental health, 23
   mental health challenges, 25
   overreliance on technology, 25
   pragmatic career decisions, 25
   unique to, 25
   work-life balance, 23
Gerber, Scott, 69
Gerstner Jr., Louis V., 113
Gerstner, Lou, 114

Get on Board, 180
Ginsburg, Ruth Bader, 104, 139
Giorgi. Cesere, 169
Girls Who Code clubs, 5–8
Gladwell, Malcolm, 147
goal, 9
   daily actions, 12
   directed behavior, 16
   identification, 11
   mid-career growth peak, 87
   and milestones, 12
   SMART, 61–62
   stretch, setting up, 11–12
   visualization, 12
Gokey, Tim, 78
Goldman Sachs, 191, 195
Goleman, Daniel, 54
Google, 7, 45, 123
Gorman, James, 109–112
governance, 189
Graham, Benjamin, 56
Grant, Adam, 51
Graziosi, Dean, 39–41
Greatness Code formula, 28, 196
Greatness Objective, 3
grit, 18, 20
   beyond career, 107–108
   inspiration in others, 140
   lifelong learning in
      sustaining, 100–101
   and long-term success, 157–158
   mindfulness in, 155
   in peak-stage leader, 108–109
   and social capital, 23
   unbalanced, 153
Grit: The Power of Passion and Perseverance (2018), 5

growth
   enduring power of, 136
   legacy of, 132, 135
   mindset, 15, 17, 130, 136
GTO processes, 78
Guarino, Christofer, xvii–xviii

H
habits, 157, 173, 201
   stacking, 125, 129, 130, 137, 153, 157
Haggard,. Merle, 13, 14
The Handbook of Board Governance, 180
hard work, 49, 53, 73
   Baby Boomers, 23
Harris, Carla, 49
Hastings, Reed, 122
health
   evaluation, 176
   mid-career growth peak, 88
   role in retirement timing, 175
healthcare consultants and
      retirement plan, 178
Heath, Edward, 43
Hoffman, Reid, 68
Huffington, Arianna, 152
The Huffington Post, 152

I
IBM, 113
ICARD process, 69–70
ICE (Intercontinental exchange), xii, xiii, xv, 105, 106
impulse control, 18
inclusive leadership, 118
Industrial Revolution, 20

industry events participation, 187
influence, 72–73, 142, 144–145, 150
innovation, 23, 28, 77, 112, 124, 125
   AWS story, 125
   at mid-career stage, 73–74
Inspire1Million campaign, 53
Instagram, 46, 143
   social capital in, 47
intelligence, 198
intelligence quotient (IQ), 54
Interactive Data Corp (IDC), 105
Intercontinental Exchange (ICE), 105
investments, early, 46
investors, 46
Islam, Sabirul, 51–53
Iwerks, Ub, 31, 48

J
Jackley, Jessica, 149
job market, 23
   Millennials challenges, 24
Jobs, Steve, 132, 157
Jurek, Scott, 156

K
King, Jr., Martin Luther, 145–146
Kiva Microfunds, 149
knowledge sharing and mentorship, 143–144
Korn Ferry, 10–12, 18, 54, 118, 132
Krieger, Mike, 45, 47

L
leaders, grit inspiring, 115
leadership, 107
   effective, 119
   inclusive, 118
   persistent, 111
   social capital in, 119
Leblanc, Richard, 180
legacy, 104
   definition of, 140
   ethical leadership on, 144–145
   impact measurement, 145–146
   social capital in, 141
   strategies for, 146
lifelong learning, 119
   by Ron Moultrie, 126–129
   stamina and passion, 127
   in sustaining grit, 100–101
LinkedIn, 68
   profile, 186
London International Financial Futures and Options Exchange (LIFFE), 105
London Stock Exchange Group (LSEG), 191, 193, 195
loyalty, 22, 23
Luzzara, Marco, 169

M
management principle, 18
marital adjustments, 177
Marshall Plan for Moms, 7
Martin, Lynn, 104–107
Mastermind Business System, 40
Mastermind.com, 40
Matterhorn, 28–30
McCann, Jim, 126
McRaven, William H., 115
mental health
   acceptance of, 155
   challenges, 154
   Gen Z, 23, 25

mental toughness, 87
mentor, 56
mentorship, 57, 188
   and knowledge sharing, 143–144
   opportunities, Gen Xers, 27
Mickey Mouse, 48
Microsoft, 7, 102, 123
mid-career stage, 67, 76
   connector, 68–70
   and COVID-19 pandemic, 75
   grit and growth, 74
   innovation at, 73–74
   market values, 93
   passion, 93
   peak growth, 87–89
   persistence, 73–74
   playbook, 91–96
   unique access, 93
   world-class quadrant, 93
milestones
   celebration and mid-career growth, 89
   and goal, 12, 53, 75, 95, 103, 176
Millennials (Gen Y), 19
   burnout, from overcommitment, 24
   career, 23
   emotional intelligence gaps, 24
   financial challenges, 24
   gender pay disparities, 24
   generalizations, 23
   high expectations, purpose-driven work, 24
   impatience, rapid career growth, 23
   job market challenges, 24
   job market saturation, 24
   negative stereotypes, 24
   struggles with workplace hierarchies, 24
   unique to, 25
Miller, G.E., 18
mindfulness, 87, 103, 137
   in balancing grit, 155
mindset
   beginner's, 101
   flexible, 122
   growth, 17, 130
Moms First organization, 7
morning routines, 10, 31, 115
motivation, 54
   intrinsic, 199
Moultrie, Ron, 126–129
Munger, Charlie, 31, 72
music, 13

N

National Association of Corporate Directors (NACD) templates, 180
National Women's Day publication, 132–135
Neff, Kristin, 156
negative stereotypes, Millennials, 24
Netflix, 122
networking, 49
   challenges with, 26
   digital, 22
   expansion with intention, 62
   and social capital, 26
   strategic, 47, 62
neural adaptation, 17
neural plasticity, 17
Nooyi, Indra, 131, 144
nutrition, 149, 156
NYSE Group, 105

O

One Woman's Army: A Black Officer Remembers the WAC, 82
Ongania, Enrico, 169
operating partners, 184
operational expertise, 188
operational setbacks, 111
opportunity, 122–123, 132
Orr, Evelyn, 132
overreliance on technology, Gen Z, 25
oxytocin-based systems, 199

P

partner role, 188
part-time work, 176
passion, 15, 35–36, 58, 102, 192, 194, 199
  mid-career growth peak, 88
Paugh, Ryan, 69
pay-as-you-go model, 124
Pay Up: The Future of Women and Work (and Why It's Different Than You Think), 7
peak-career professionals, 159–163
people agility, 49
PepsiCo, 131, 144
Perna, Tom, 200–201
Perry, Chris, 28–35, 78
persistence, 15, 17, 34–35, 38, 58, 192, 193, 199
personal brand, 67, 71
  board level, 180
  building, 72
  crafting, 61
  with PE and VC, 186
Peter, Laurence J., 18

Picasso, Pablo, 101
pivot
  faith-based, 149
  real-life, 148–149
  steps to, 148
Polman, Paul, 145
Pond, Mossy, 87
post-career, 167–168 *see also* retirement
post-World War II era, 20
pre-retirement counseling, 175 *see also* retirement
private equity (PE), 183, 185
problem-solving, 17, 34, 84
progress, 34–35
ProxyVote™, 78
public company board service, 179
public service, 142
purpose
  mid-career growth peak, 88
  Millennials, 24

Q

5Qs, 191
  authenticity, 118
  and social capital, 20
  social capital in leadership, 118
  strategies for cultivating, 116

R

Randolph, Marc, 122
reframing setbacks, 38
regulatory landscape, 111
reinforcement, 18
Relia-COBOL™, 77, 78
research firms, 185

resilience, 6–7, 15, 16, 34, 52–53, 58, 192, 193
  mid-career growth peak, 87
  physical health in, 156–157
  psychological, 17
  through change, 131–132
  through letting go, 199–200
  through self-compassion, 156
retirement *see also* public company board service
  challenges and plan for solutions, 177
  coaches and retirement plan, 178
  components of, 178
  financial plan, 178
  flexible options, 176
  healthcare plan, 178
  income, 173
  legacy plan, 178
  lifestyle plan, 178
  planning, 172–178
  retired executives, 184
  timing with personal goals, 176
  trial run, 175
  withdrawal strategy, 173
  written plan, 177
Rifkin, Adam, 69
Robbins, Tony, 39
Roberts, Alfred, 42
Rolet, Xavier, 131
Rowling, J. K., 38

S
Salesforce, 155
Saujani, Reshma, 5–8
Scalia, Antonin, 140
Schwimmer, David, 193
Schifellite, Bob, 79
sector experts, 184
sector-specific firms, 185
Seery, M.D., 17
self-awareness, 18, 19, 54, 55
  and development, 118
self-compassion, 156
self-criticism, 156
self-inquiry, 92
self-reflection, 129–130
self-regulation, 54, 55
semi-retired professional, 179
serve on boards, post-career, 172
setbacks
  AWS overcoming, 124
  in career, 44
  operational, 111
  reframing, 38
short-term consulting, 188
sleep, 152, 156, 157
small world network, 68
SMART goals, 61–62
  mid-career stage, 96
Smart Is Not Enough, 54, 71
social capital, 4, 9, 21, 22
  early career challenges, 40
  emotional intelligence as catalyst, 55
  foundation of, 50–51
  goal of, 57
  and grit, 23
  in Instagram's success, 47
  in leadership, 119
  in legacy, 141
  leverage of, 74–75
  network, 13
  network resources and, 47

social capital (*continued*)
  as peak-level leader, 116–119
  and 5Qs, 20
social isolation, 177
social learning theory, 18
social skills, 54, 55
Sprecher, Jeff, 106
stamina, 15, 34, 58, 102, 192, 194
Stanley, Morgan, 109–112
Stevenson, Jane Edison, 132
Stewart, Gary, 13
The Story of Success (2008), 147
strategic alliances, 72–73
strategic oversight, 188
strategic planning, 94
stress management, 18
stretch goal, setting up, 11–12
struggles
  with adaptation, Gen X, 26
  with workplace
    hierarchies, Gen Y, 24
Superconnector, 69
sustaining effort, 17
sustaining growth
  self-reflection in, 129–130
  strategies for, 137
Systrom, Kevin, 45, 47

T
teaching roles, post-career, 172
Tennessee Whiskey: The Dean Dillon Story, 14
Tenore, Haley, 155
Thatcher, Margaret, 41–43
time management, 88

Truman, Harry, 83
trust, 55
  and collaboration, 144
2024 Paris Olympics, 154
2021 Tokyo Olympics, 154
twisties, 154
Twitter, 46

U
Unilever, 145

V
value, during engagements, 188
venture capital (VC), 183, 185
Vince, Robin, xiii, xv
Virgin Group, 100
visualization
  exercise, 160
  goal, 12

W
Weber, Charles, 77
well-being, 151
  mindfulness in, 155
Who Says Elephants Can't Dance? (2003), 114
Winfrey, Oprah, 71, 103, 143–144
Women's Army Auxiliary Corps (WAAC), 81
Wood, John, 148
work-life balance, Gen Z, 23
workplace hierarchies, Millennials, 24
World Health Organization, 153
World War II, 20

YOU'VE CRACKED THE CODE.

Visit GreatnessCode.com to put the formula to work with:

Videos

Resources

Engagements

and more

GreatnessCode.com